WHY NOT ME?

A Roadmap to Turning Setbacks into Success and Living Your Best Life

BY SCOTT TENNANT

For Keith
Our relationship is my biggest success.

Copyright Information

Title: Why Not Me? A Roadmap to Turning Setbacks into Success and Living Your Best Life

Author: Scott Tennant

Publisher: Bordista Press

ISBN: 978-0-9968876-4-9

Library of Congress Classification: BF637.S8

Dewey Decimal Classification: 158.1

Printed in the United States of America

First Edition

Disclaimer

The information provided in this book is for educational purposes only and does not constitute legal, financial, or business advice. Readers are encouraged to consult with a qualified professional for advice specific to their situation.

Contact Information

- Website: scott-tennant.com
- Email: stennant@senergy.us
- Social Media:
    - LinkedIn   http://www.linkedin.com/in/scott-tennant-6a4b445
    - Instagram   scottetennant

TABLE OF CONTENTS

FOREWORD BY GERI JEWELL

I first met Scott in 2014 in Sedona at The World Wisdom Days conference. I had performed the night before, not knowing that he was in my audience.

Later that evening, returning to my room, I got news that my friend (David Zimmerman) had a heart attack. I immediately thought of the sacred Hopi Prayer Bell that was placed onstage that night for those who wished to place a written prayer in the slot under the bell. I figured I could do it in the morning, before my workshop. However my workshop was canceled. I was bummed, but it turned out to be a blessing in disguise. The Prayer Bell had been moved near a gift shop. Since I had a free day, I had my escort take me there to place my prayer for David.

Unknown to me, Scott was also there with his friend and co-worker, Karla. She had spotted me at the Prayer Bell, and said to Scott "I know you are very disappointed that you didn't get to meet Geri Jewell last evening, but just turn around..."

And that is when Scott and I connected, at the Prayer Bell in Sedona, Arizona. Having met, I knew intuitively I we were meant to be friends, and I spontaneously told my escort that she was leaving me in good hands with Scott, Keith and Karla. She assumed we all knew each other and left. However, I had never met these people before and trusted that the Universe was guiding us.

"

We were hungry, but none of us knew our way around Sedona. It seemed as though we drove around for about an hour or so before we found a place to eat. None of us knew where we were, but we had our late lunch, enjoying our newfound friendship. On our way back to the Hotel, after spending roughly three hours together, we were running out of gas, having no idea where a gas station was. But we made it, with the gas on empty. We were driving with a full tank of faith. Our friendship was sealed.

We spoke by phone afterwards, and about three months later I was asked to speak at The White House. Of course, there were many close friends I could have asked to go with me, but for some reason I thought of Scott.

So now our friendship was further cemented by our shared experience in Washington D.C. We were instant friends and then met up again in Sedona the following year. Only this time, adding Norman Lear and my sister Gloria to the equation.

Gloria was my younger sister, but extremely protective of me. I had told her all about Scott, and now they were going to meet each other for the first time. It was fairly late, and Gloria & I were hungry. We found one restaurant open, and lo & behold, Scott and Keith were sitting at the bar! Pulling a chair out for me, Scott said he wanted to sit next to his sister. Gloria said, but Geri is MY sister. Laughing I introduced them, saying that I could be a sister to both.

Scott introduced himself to Gloria, and she said that she knew exactly who he was, that she extensively researched him, and concluded that he was okay. She had questioned many other people that had used me over the years, and she didn't want that to happen again.

It was a magical weekend, as I opened for the keynote speaker, Norman Lear, who by the way, discovered me decades prior, casting me as Cousin Geri on the NBC series, The Facts of Life.

What no one knew at that time, was two year later Gloria was diagnosed with lung cancer. It was the most devastating time for me in my entire life, and upon her death six months later, my fieriest protector was gone. There was no reason to trust my brother-in-law to look after me, so I turned to Scott (my new little brother) who Gloria approved of two years prior.

Scott is an earth angel in more ways than one, and we were always on the same spiritual wavelength. So, when I asked him look after me the way Gloria had done for her entire life, his attitude was, "Why not me?" He loved me and knew I needed the added support in my life.

I believe that there are no accidents in life, and situations and circumstances will unfold the way they are meant to be as long as we never confuse power with force. If we have to force something to happen, it is ego driven, and spiritual power moves to the back burner waiting for our attentive hearts again.

My journey with Scott was never forced. It was spontaneous and moved along in life as we were carried by invisible wings of love, laughter and light. In trusting the universe, our trust in one another has only deepened, and both of us have acknowledged the power in living with the attitude of "why not me?" instead of "why me?"

Love,

Geri Jewell

actress, stand-up comedian, diversity consultant, and motivational speaker

INTRODUCTION

Words and thoughts have power—massive power over your mind, body, and spirit. I learned this very early in my life. I was born blessed with young parents, high school sweethearts from McGregor, Texas, a little town not too far from the "big city" Waco. It seemed like the perfect setup for a great life: a small, fairly open-minded town where everyone knew everyone—and, yes, everything—around them. There was, however, a fatal flaw in this fairy tale. At age seven, my father, Joe Don, was diagnosed with juvenile diabetes. This was considered a death sentence at the time. It was the early '60s, and his doctors didn't expect him to live past thirteen.

I never heard anyone in my immediate family say, "I can't do it"– something I doubt many people can say about their own families. The news of her son's impending death didn't stop my grandmother, Janice. She was a constant reader and started to study and act on what she found to save her son. She created a lifestyle focused on good food, exercise, and nutritional supplementation. She and my grandfather told young Joe Don to go and live to the fullest. Joe Don grew long past his life expectancy and became a self-confident, open-minded, and smart young man. He learned quickly that life is short and could end at any moment.

Joe Don married my mom, Marilyn, just out of high school. By all accounts, they were meant for each other. Together they raised me in an environment of love, openness, and knowing that every day must be the best day ever. Holidays, birthdays, anniversaries, and even small events had to be perfect, epic, and filled with life lessons.

I somehow knew that my life was a bit different from a typical child's. We would travel to bigger cities than Waco with my dad's work. Other children would have a "wrangler" or an activities program. Most of the time, though, I would be dressed up and taken with the adults. I had gotten to interact with adults from a very early age, which allowed me to spend time with them in their groups and in places most kids don't have access to. We often joked that I had been to the Playboy Club four to five times before I was even twelve.

The members-only venue, which required an actual key to get into, was surprisingly sophisticated, with no nudity or touching allowed, and more of a multi-room wonderland where sophistication met entertainment. The Bunnies, with their iconic ears and tails, moved through the crowd with grace and professionalism. As an eight-year-old in a suit sitting with adults, I was treated with the same respect as everyone else, with maybe a bit more attention from the bunnies. The place had this magical energy—you'd see Dallas Cowboys players at one table and famous musicians at another, all while enjoying world-class performances in an atmosphere where everyone felt special, even a kid like me who was just soaking it all in.

As I grew, many other wonderful adventures would appear, and we would step into them with joy, learning, and growth. I attended business meetings where executives would explain complex deals to me as if I were a colleague. I was invited backstage at concerts to meet musicians who were surprised by my knowledge of their careers. I traveled to art galleries in Houston where curators would take time to explain the history behind masterpieces to a curious young boy. These opportunities showed me how I could make a difference in the world. My parents worked hard to fulfill their wish to give me meaningful experiences before Dad was no longer around to give them.

But that day did come. I was twelve years old. It was a sudden jolt into reality.

The world I had known—filled with adventure, learning, and my father's guiding presence—shifted beneath my feet. One moment I was a child being groomed for greatness, and the next I was facing a future without one of my greatest teachers. The loss of my Father was immense, but the foundation that my parents had built was strong. Every lesson, every experience, every conversation with those adults in rooms I shouldn't have been in—it all suddenly made sense. They weren't just adventures; they were preparation.

Was I prepared? Was I good enough? Could I survive? What was to come? It was time to step up and be a man for my mom. At twelve.

The journey had only just begun. I knew I was prepared, good enough, and that I could survive, but I looked around and wondered how I could do it. Why me? Other kids got to play with abandon, their youth still intact. But other kids hadn't had the experiences I had, they didn't have a dad who had prepared them just for this moment. Yes, the journey was only beginning, but I would carry the blessing of my parents' legacy with me. I would follow in their footsteps, living fully and loving deeply.

I turned the question of "Why me?" into "Why not me?" – and eventually that question became an empowering phrase: "Why not me!" This became my guiding light. Through every challenge, every opportunity, and every crossroads, I would return to these three words. They weren't just a motto—they were a mindset that transformed how I approached life's obstacles. And in the pages that follow, I'll show you how this simple phrase can become your foundation too, helping you turn your own setbacks into steppingstones for success.

PART ONE

CONCEIVE

Why Are You Here?

There are a few things I know about you already. First, you're a seeker—someone who's constantly looking for answers. Second, you're socially conscious and self-aware, and you understand the impact you have on the world. Most importantly, you're excited to do the work. You know that the more awake you are, the faster you move toward the life you want to live.

Does that sound like you? If it does, you're my kind of person.

But let's not sugarcoat it. You didn't get to this place without walking through the weeds. I know your journey hasn't been all sunshine and roses. You've taken hits—hardships, oppression, rejection. You've worked tirelessly to be where you are now. But though you've made it this far, you're still wondering what's next, and thinking even deeper: *WHY*?

I get it. As an openly gay man growing up in Texas in the '80s with the last name of Fagg, I've had my own share of grit to chew. The kind of experiences that make you grow up faster than you should and teach you how to read a room before your feet even cross the threshold. I know what it's like to look around and ask, "Why me?" Not in the pitying kind of way—but a bone-deep plea for the universe to make some damn sense.

This book is going to ask you to face that question—not to be swallowed by it, but to turn it on its head. To change "Why me?" into "Why not me?" and eventually "Why not me!" Because the truth is, if you don't start asking better questions, you'll keep living by the wrong answers.

To start, I want you to reconnect with your why. That part of you that existed long before the world put you in a box. The part that still dares to dream even while reality drags you down. The whisper that says, "more is possible," even when you're too tired to believe it.

You're not here by accident. And no, you don't need a flashy sign or some five-step plan to confirm it. Just a bit of honesty and the courage to ask the better question.

So, let's begin.

Why Am I Here?

I've asked myself this more than once—not just why I'm here in this world, but why do I feel pulled to write any of this down? And to be honest, I pushed back. For a long time, I figured someone smarter, shinier, or with a few more letters after their name might be better suited, someone who hadn't been knocked around quite so much.

But getting knocked around teaches you things that clean resumes never could. It teaches you how to stand back up, even when you're bitter about it. After all, spite can be a powerful tool for motivation. Being knocked around shows you how to feel things deeply, and how to recognize someone else's scars because they're on you as well.

I grew up in a small south Texas town in the Bible Belt. I was shy, self-conscious, and a little chunky. You already know that my birth dad, Joe Don, had been diagnosed with juvenile diabetes at seven and doctors said he wouldn't live past thirteen. Every day, both in his life and mine, was shaped by the pressure that "Today has to be the best day, since tomorrow may never come." While it led to amazing adventures, it also placed a lot of pressure on me as a young child.

And then there was my last name, Fagg. "Two G's," we'd always mention. But in that small town, the nuance didn't matter, especially because others perceived me as gay from a young age. I literally grew up a Fagg. People called me that from the time I was old enough to understand what hate sounded like. It taught me to stay small. Careful. Strategic. I watched how I walked, talked, behaved, and where to keep my gaze. Even just appearing to "look at a man" below their eyes could cause trouble, no matter the reasoning. I became hyper-aware of where the exits were. If older boys were around, I knew it was safer just to leave. I could see their contempt and hatred. They were talking about me, the Fagg in the room.

School wasn't much better. It bored me to tears. Teachers accused me of being a know-it-all when I pointed out textbook inaccuracies or challenged outdated assumptions. I wasn't trying to be difficult—I had been raised to think critically, to engage. So much of my childhood had been spent traveling alongside my dad, experiencing diverse cities, and talking with businessmen who took the time to explain what they were meeting about and why. But in school where conformity was expected, curiosity was punished.

When my mom and I had the chance to move to a bigger city, I hesitated. I'd dreamed of escaping McGregor, but I also knew how to survive there. I knew the rules. Safety, even miserable safety, is hard to leave. I was scared. I'd spent my life burdened by an inner voice that told me, "You're a Fagg! A Fag! A short, overweight, shy, and self-conscious fag!" Ultimately, I decided to stay in my hometown. At just fourteen, I wasn't ready to uproot and leave what was familiar, especially right after my father had died.

Instead, I commuted between my hometown and Houston, living with my aunt and uncle while I finished school. Only ten years older than me, my aunt and uncle were more like older siblings. They were young and vibrant and treated me with love and compassion. They allowed me to grow into who I wanted to be, to speak openly, and to strive for greatness. They became like second parents, the respect and trust between us were like a mirror to my mom and dad's.

That part of my life taught me so much that I still carry with me today. Driving across the state for four and a half hours (each way) was hard. I had to plan accordingly. With a hardship license, credit card, and a car I maintained myself, I carried all my fear and baggage with me.

But I also carried my dreams. Dreams I was starting to make come true.

What had changed wasn't my odds of success as a gay kid in a small town whose father had just died—it was me. I stopped waiting for things around me to change and worked on how I could change myself. I knew God had bigger plans for me, but it took opening my eyes to see them.

I didn't come here to hand out glossy inspiration or play the part of some guru who lives a perfect life. That's not me. And frankly, I've heard enough of those talks to know I wouldn't want to keep reading if this book had that tone. What I know is what I've lived. What I've fought, tooth and nail, to learn and unlearn. And under all the noise, I found truth. Not the capital-T kind—just mine.

So, if you're wondering why I'm here writing this—it's because I believe, deep in my bones, that if I speak from that honest, scarred-up place, maybe it'll spark something in you too. Not to do what I do. But to remember who you are and what you want from life. And maybe, just maybe, if we stop pretending, we have to be polished before we show up, we might finally start showing up as we are. Real.

What not you?

Why not me?

Why not us, exactly as we were born to be.

Why Not You?

My journey from being that scared kid in a small Texas town to the person writing this book wasn't linear. It was filled with moments where I had to choose between shrinking or expanding. Between accepting limitations or challenging them. The most powerful tool I discovered along the way wasn't a strategy or a secret—it was a question that became a declaration. A question that can transform your life too.

"What do you want to do when you grow up?" I was fourteen when my stepdad, Dr. Jerry Tennant, MD, asked me this. He was a famous ophthalmic surgeon at the time, and I was only just beginning my journey to self-discovery, so the question felt a bit forward.

My first answer was something like, "I will own my own business, make lots of money, drive exotic cars, make movies, and live in a mansion while traveling the world." Dad went on to explain that a life like that doesn't come so easily. I would have to make a plan for myself, study hard in school, graduate from a great college, and then work harder to establish myself in my chosen career. At the time, I wasn't sure if I believed him. I knew plenty of people who had taken easier paths but still became highly successful. I decided right then and there that I could find my own path forward too.

When people doubted me or that little voice inside of my head started to ask, "why me?", I would reply with a strong resounding "why not me!" Notice that I used an exclamation mark. It's not a question. It's a declaration. A mindset. It's one of my strongest beliefs that nobody's opinion of you matters more than your own. If anyone's ever going to stand up for you, it's got to be you. You are your own best advocate. Only you can make change happen for yourself. My goal with this book is to help you tell yourself, "Why not me!" and start carving a new path to your own idea of success.

This is where the power to conceive begins. When you declare 'Why not me!' you're planting the first seed of possibility. You're creating space in your mind for a new reality—one where you're not defined by others' expectations or your past struggles. This is the first step in our Conceive, Believe, Receive framework. Before you can believe in something or receive it, you must first conceive it as possible for you.

The moment I conceived a different future for myself at fourteen, something shifted. I didn't have all the answers. I didn't know exactly how I'd get there. But I had created mental permission to imagine myself succeeding on my own terms. That's the gift I want to give you through these pages—permission to conceive a life beyond what others have told you is possible.

I've since accomplished all of the things I told my stepdad I wanted that day at fourteen, and then some. As I'm sure you have accomplished more than anyone thought you could. Now, we're here to go even deeper into your desires and claim even more of that "why not me!" energy.

Why Not Me! Reflection Exercise

Take a moment to connect with your own "Why not me!" power:

- **Identify Your Victories:** In your journal, list at least five times when you overcame someone else's doubt or your own self-limiting beliefs. What did you accomplish that surprised even you?
- **Name Your Declarations:** Write down three areas of your life where you need to shift from "Why me?" to "Why not me!" Be specific about what you want to achieve.

- **Create Your Permission Slip:** Write yourself a permission slip that begins with "I give myself permission to..." Fill in the blank with the dreams you've been hesitant to claim.
- Speak It Out Loud: Stand in front of a mirror and practice saying, "Why not me!" with conviction. Notice how your posture and energy change when you declare these words rather than question them.

Remember, conceiving new possibilities isn't about having all the answers—it's about opening the door to questions that expand rather than limit you. Your journey begins with giving yourself permission to imagine a different outcome.

Claim Your Desires

"QUALITY QUESTIONS CREATE A QUALITY LIFE. SUCCESSFUL PEOPLE ASK BETTER QUESTIONS, AND AS A RESULT, THEY GET BETTER ANSWERS."

– TONY ROBBINS

You've heard it before: 'Dream big!' 'Think outside the box!' I've heard these phrases my entire life. But the truth is, desire—real, aligned desire—requires something deeper than just making a wish and hoping it comes true. It requires integrity.

You see, ego is a dream killer. It inflates our pride and makes us feel superior to others. Ego wants self-worth to be proven. It stems from comparison, not from clarity. And it can cause us to ignore the negative side of karma.

Karma isn't just the bad stuff that loops back around when we've messed up. Karma is alignment. Good things, like blessings, gifts, and opportunities, flow more freely–and are more easily seen and acknowledged–when we approach life from a place of positivity and gratitude.

When our goals are warped by ego, they're not in service of ourselves or others. Instead, they're set with a kind of ill intent. We might think we want that car, that job, that partner, but if the core intent is to *LOOK* successful or *FEEL* superior, we're setting ourselves up to fail—or worse, to get exactly what we asked for and still feel empty.

This is why it's important to shape your desires around gratitude and love. Trust me on this one. When you understand that your success doesn't have to come from someone else's failure, your desire becomes an offering instead of a demand. You begin to work with the universe, rather than fight against it.

Each day when I wake up, I ask myself: "Who am I supposed to meet today, and what miracles can I actively create with that person?" This one question, my "primary question" as Tony Robbins calls it, is one of the most powerful things I do to start my day. I become more reflective and aware, and I carry that feeling through the rest of my day. There is more meaning in my encounters as if God is placing them purposefully in my path.

Sometimes, it's not someone new. Sometimes the answer to this question is a person I've known for years. God will show me new insight into this person, allowing me to discover a new purpose behind our meeting.

Once you've learned to align your desire with positive intention, you can now build upon that foundation with clarity and purpose.

You must be at once unambiguous with what you hope to achieve and open to having it come to you in unexpected ways. I say this from experience. You've likely been told, "Be careful what you wish for; you just might get it." There's a reason why that is. I've wished for things and gotten them, exactly as I described, and I realized quickly why I should have considered them more carefully. My friends laugh and stop me when I start to say, "I wish I had...."

"Are you a thousand percent sure?" They ask. "You know you may just get your wish." So, I've learned to rephrase, refine, and re-align my wishes, not to specific exact timing and details, but to precise and explicit feelings and experiences I want to have. Let me share a personal example that taught me how powerfully our perspective can shape what we see in the world.

While writing this book, I started to get overwhelmed with the details of the process. I was focusing on the process of promoting and publishing before I'd even finished writing it. I was feeling vulnerable from the stories in here and really struggling with writer's block to get more out. I had always been taught that if you hustle harder you can make anything happen, but my writing coach, Lauren Marie Fleming, reminded me that creativity doesn't work that way. "You can't draw from an empty well," she reminded me, and—in her writing dominatrix style that is both firm and loving—forbid me from touching my book for a month. Instead, she assigned me the job of filling my creative bucket.

This shift in perspective changed everything. Instead of seeing time away from writing as "not working" or "falling behind," I began to see it as an essential part of the creative process. By changing how I looked at rest—from an indulgence to a necessity—I transformed my relationship with creativity. When I returned to writing after that month, the words flowed more easily because I had changed what I was looking for. I wasn't searching for ways to force productivity; I was discovering the natural rhythm of creation that includes both action and rest.

Not only was it this beautiful reminder that love was all around me, but it was also a moment to look back at why I wanted to write a book in the first place. Yes, I want to share my experiences and expertise to connect with you, the reader, and aid you on your journey. But I also decided to work with Lauren because I knew I needed creativity in my life again. My house is covered in art, including pieces my husband and I had made together, and yet I wasn't making time for it in my life anymore. I'd worked so hard to build myself up as a businessman, that I'd forgotten how much I loved to play.

Lauren was constantly telling me that the journey of discovering yourself and your voice while writing a book is as important as the final thing, and by filling my life with creativity simply because it was something I loved, I was reminded, once again, that she was right. After a month of creative exploration without productivity expectations, I was able to come back to my book and see it through the eyes of art and play, and that made all the difference in how I could give it my heart and soul.

I have worked hard to build a life centered around what I want to be. Years have passed where I had to make choices, both simple and hard, to surround myself with people who inspire me to be greater while loving me for who I am. I have learned how art, music and movies affect the way I see the world and see myself. I've discovered how I can control how I am affected by all these things by deciding who and what I allow into my space.

This is what happens when we shift our perspective. We literally begin to see different opportunities, different patterns, different possibilities. You become what you seek, what you think, and what you wish for. Your perspective is shaped by how you listen, what you watch, and who you choose to surround yourself with. If you believe you are worthy, you will be. We are connected to and affected by everything around us. It is how we choose to interact with it all that shapes our reality.

Create Your Mantra

MAN·TRA • NOUN • A WORD OR PHRASE USED IN MEDITATION AS A TOOL TO HELP FOCUS AND CALM THE MIND.

A mantra is more than just something you say, it's a tuning fork for your soul. It's a way to bring yourself back to your purpose, help you focus, steady emotions, or boost awareness.

Each day, I begin with a ritual. Using all my senses, I set up a space that invites me into the mindset of gratitude. It reminds me that the little things matter. I start with lighting a prayer candle, infused with essential oil. This brings a soft light to my office (sight), and a calming scent (smell). With this, I say a small prayer for love, acceptance, expression, creativity, and success. Mantras from around the world are woven into music played from a SiriusXM station (sound). I sip on a freshly brewed cup of tea or coffee (taste), while I listen. It's a peaceful, slow moment that helps to ground me. And as I wait for my computer to wake up, I recite my own mantra, ready to start my day.

I've learned that when I keep the candle burning and the music playing throughout the day, I stay in a more meditative state. It's become a part of my ritual now, acting as a gentle reminder that I am safe, loved, and present. This is a day I've chosen to live, and I get to shape how it unfolds.

With daily repetition, these rituals become muscle memory. Like a dancer on Broadway rehearsing their steps until the movements come naturally and without thought. The body remembers. The heart stays open. Your brain will naturally return to peace, love, and joy, no matter where you are or what happens around you. This is how you train your state of being—not by forcing control, but by tending to what is sacred.

When you consistently live in this space, that is when you finally get to create. This is where the power of conception truly begins. Your mantra becomes the seed from which new possibilities grow. It clears away the mental clutter and limiting beliefs that block your vision, allowing you to see opportunities you might otherwise miss. In this clarity, you can name your desires with precision and listen for your next step without the static of doubt or fear. Be specific and stay purposeful. Your mantra doesn't just calm your mind—it prepares fertile ground where your dreams can take root. You CAN Conceive, Believe, and Receive your dreams exactly as you wish—like a genie in a bottle. True manifestation becomes more possible than ever, once you master this state of being. Your mantra is the first whisper of what you're calling into existence.

Craft Your Personal Mantra

Find a quiet moment and reflect on what you most need right now. Is it courage? Peace? Clarity? Focus? Let this need guide your mantra's purpose.

Keep it simple and positive. Your mantra should be short enough to remember easily—typically 3-10 words. Frame it in the present tense as if it's already true: "I am..." rather than "I will be..."

Make it personal and meaningful. Your mantra should resonate with you emotionally. It might be:

- A statement of truth: "I am enough exactly as I am"
- A reminder of purpose: "I create value in everything I touch"
- A declaration of intent: "I choose peace over perfection"

Create your ritual space. Engage your senses as much as possible.

- Visual: A candle, a special spot, or a meaningful object
- Sound: Calming music or silence
- Scent: Essential oils or incense

- Touch: A comfortable position or a special item to hold
- Taste: Tea, coffee, or water to sip mindfully

Practice daily. Repeat your mantra during your morning ritual for at least 21 days. Notice how it begins to shape your thoughts and actions throughout the day.

Your mantra is more than words—it's the foundation of what you're conceiving for your life. Choose it with intention, practice it with consistency, and watch as it helps you create the mindset needed to manifest your deepest desires.

So choose your mantra. Light your candle. And begin.

Are You Gifted Enough to Gift?

I remember when I first met Shann. She was quiet, clinging to the edges of the room like a classic wallflower, a simple blue sketchbook tucked under one arm.

I was hosting a dinner party with fifty or so guests, all of whom were open-minded and successful individuals. It was an event to connect, not impress. Where artists, thinkers, dreamers, and doers could come together and share their stories. Somehow, in the hum of voices and clinking glasses, Shann found the courage to walk over to me.

Introducing herself, she said she usually avoided speaking to new people. That she mostly kept to her family.

I asked, "Then why'd you approach me?"

She paused, her face flushing before she said, "You seemed approachable. And... because you're somebody.'"

I laughed. Not to mock her, but because I remember what it felt like to keep myself small, to believe my voice didn't matter.

I told her, "You are somebody too!" and she giggled.

I explained that I was once just like her. Believing it was rude and intrusive to approach others, you know, growing up in the South where you were expected to only speak if spoken to.

Cutting through the small talk, I asked her, "What does your soul want you to do?"

She hesitated. Then said quietly, "I'm an artist. But I don't like to share it. It's just some lines on paper and that's it."

"Just lines?" I smiled. "Let me see?" Her hands tightened around her sketchbook, reluctant to part with it.

We stood in my foyer, where I kept much of my collected works of art on display. I gestured to them and said, "I purchased these pieces because I either know the artist personally or am familiar with their life story. Each canvas, each sculpture, is an expression—a small window into the artist's experience. I feel connected to the artist in this way. Their decision to share these expressions is what brings us closer together as humans. They are gifts."

She opened her sketchbook and showed me the renderings that she had been working on. They were incredible, far beyond "just lines." Some of them looked ready for a gallery wall. Others seemed to have a life of their own like they were waiting to be worn, held, or passed down.

I asked her, "What did you decide to show me?"

She replied, "Do you think my sketches are gifts? That's something my mom has always said."

"Of course they are!" I told her. "But the question is—are you gifted enough to gift?"

Her brow furrowed and I could tell the phrase hadn't landed yet, so I continued. "Gifting doesn't mean being the best. It doesn't mean perfecting something before it leaves your hands. It means SHARING. Sharing your voice, your view, your expression, your questions. When someone sees your lines and they FEEL something, that's a gift. When they ask what your art means, and you share the story, that's the gift. When your work becomes part of someone else's world, and they see something of themselves in it—that exchange is what is sacred."

You see, YOU arc the gift! The expression of your experiences, of your growth, creates opportunities for connection and communication that are unique for both the artist and the viewer. Your gift is the raindrop that starts the ripple. When we deny this part of ourselves, we deny ourselves and others the opportunity to witness, reflect, grow, and be changed.

So dust off the thing you've hidden. Sketch it. Say it. Sing it. Offer it up like a gift and trust that the right person will receive it. If it matters to you, it will matter to someone else. Out there in the world, someone is waiting for what only YOU can give.

This is where conception begins—not just in dreaming of what you might create, but in recognizing what you've already been given. Before you can conceive of new possibilities, you must first acknowledge the gifts already within you. Many of us struggle to manifest our dreams not because we lack vision, but because we've buried our innate talents under layers of doubt and fear. We conceive of grand futures while overlooking the seeds of greatness already planted within us. Your unique expression—whether it's art, insight, compassion, or expertise—is the foundation upon which all your future creations will stand. When you acknowledge your gifts and choose to share them, you're not just conceiving what might be possible someday; you're activating what's already true about you today. This recognition is often the missing piece that allows the full cycle of Conceive, Believe, Receive to unfold. The moment you see your gifts as worthy of sharing is the moment you truly begin to conceive what's possible.

Conceive, Believe, Receive Action Items:

The first step in any transformation is allowing yourself to imagine what could be. Before you can believe in a possibility or receive it into your life, you must first conceive it—see it clearly in your mind's eye, feel it in your heart, and claim it as something that could be yours. This is where your journey truly begins.

Conception isn't just about daydreaming, though that certainly has its place. It's about intentionally creating a vision that resonates with your deepest values and desires. It's about giving yourself permission to want more, to be more, to experience more than what your current circumstances might suggest is possible.

In my own life, I've found that the quality of what I conceive directly impacts what I eventually receive. When my vision was clouded by doubt or limited by what others told me was realistic, my results reflected those limitations. But when I allowed myself to conceive boldly, without the constraints of "how" or "when," doors began to open that I couldn't have anticipated.

The journey begins with conception—the moment when you first allow yourself to imagine what could be. This initial phase is about opening your mind to new possibilities and planting the seeds of your future reality. These practices will help you strengthen your ability to conceive new possibilities and prepare you for the next phases of your journey.

- **Ask Better Questions.** When faced with a challenge, reframe the problem instead of focusing on it. A better question opens the door to better answers.

o   For example, instead of asking "Why is this happening to me?" try "What is this situation teaching me?" or "How can I use this experience to grow?"

o   Reflection: What challenge are you currently facing that could benefit from a reframed question?

- **Declare Your Mantra or Mission.** Write out your "why" and declare your mission. Share it on social media or with trusted friends. Tag me in your post so I can cheer you on!

    o   With a strong enough "why," you can propel your life forward and make your dreams a reality. Review your "why" regularly to keep it fresh and evolving as you grow.

    o   Reflection: What is the deeper purpose that drives your desires and goals?

- **Share Your Gifts.** Identify your unique talents and find ways to share them. Whether through art, mentorship, or simple acts of kindness, gifting your expression invites connection and growth.

    o   Remember that your gifts don't need to be perfect to be valuable—they just need to be authentic.

    o   Reflection: What gift have you been hesitant to share that could benefit others?

As you engage with these practices, you may notice resistance arising doubts about whether you're worthy of what you desire, fears about disappointment if things don't work out, or concerns about what others might think. This resistance is normal. It's part of the process. Acknowledge it, thank it for trying to protect you, and gently set it aside as you continue to conceive your possibilities.

Remember that conception is not a one-time event but an ongoing practice. The more you exercise your capacity to imagine and claim new possibilities, the stronger this muscle becomes. Each time you conceive something new—whether it manifests exactly as you envisioned or takes an unexpected form—you're expanding your sense of what's possible.

As you practice these three steps, you're not just conceiving new possibilities—you're creating the foundation for believing in them. In Part Two, we'll explore how to nurture these seeds of conception until they grow strong enough to manifest in your life.

PART TWO

BELIEVE

From Dreaming to Doing

From the outside, I was a confident young adult. People assumed I had it all figured out. But inside? I didn't always believe what I said out loud. I didn't know who I could trust. I wasn't even sure if I trusted myself.

But I kept showing up. Because deep down, I knew there was something bigger for me. My parents had shown me what it meant to live fully and love deeply—even in the face of limited time. My father's life taught me that purpose doesn't wait. That belief, that urgency, carried me forward. But it's not enough to just want something. You have to build the foundation for it, brick by brick.

When I was building my first business, I had the vision clearly in mind. I could see what was possible. But there was a gap between that vision and my day-to-day reality that seemed impossible to cross. What I discovered was that belief isn't just about positive thinking—it's about aligning your actions, environment, and inner dialogue with what you say you want. It's about making decisions today as if your desired future is already inevitable. That's the difference between wishful thinking and true belief: one is passive hope, the other is active creation.

Part One helped you uncover the dream—that flicker of purpose, calling, or hope that says, "There's more for me." Part Two is where you will learn to believe it. Not in a surface-level kind of way, but with grounded action, heart, and soul. This is the work most people skip. The part where self-doubt creeps in, old voices start shouting, and fear tries to run the show.

But you're not "most people."

In this section, I'll show you how to bridge that gap in your own life, turning your conceived dreams into believed possibilities that you live into daily. This is the chapter where you learn to walk the talk—not perfectly, but honestly. You'll start noticing the subtle ways you sabotage yourself. You'll unlearn who you had to be to survive. And you'll build the kind of self-belief that isn't performative—it's ingrained.

There are three core places we'll work on shifting in Part 2:

- **Your Environment.** The energy around you feeds the energy within you. Choose people, spaces, and experiences that help you grow, not shrink.

- **Your Input.** What you consume—conversations, media, even background noise—becomes your inner landscape. Choose wisely.

- **Your Inner Voice.** Your self-talk can be your greatest saboteur or your strongest ally. This section teaches you how to tune into truth, not just noise.

You're not here by accident. You've already started the work by picking up this book. Now it's time to go deeper—not just to *BELIEVE* in what's possible, but to become someone who LIVES like it is.

You ready?

Let's go.

Acknowledge the Odds Are Stacked Against You - And Do It Anyway

You don't have to pretend life is perfect to live a life full of purpose. In fact, the sooner you acknowledge what's stacked against you, the freer you become to move forward.

Like my mentor, Tony Robbins says, "You can't tend to your garden simply by pretending there are no weeds." You've got to get in there, pull them up by the roots, and make space for what you want to grow. That's what we'll cover in this section: learning how to name what's hard without letting it define you.

I reached a point in my life where I needed to take a hard look at what was truly serving me. I called it my "Life Audit," and it changed everything. I examined the influences around me—the news I consumed, the relationships I maintained, the spiritual practices I followed—and asked myself one simple question: "What actually serves me?"

Every evening, I'd turn on the news out of habit. I noticed a tightening in my chest, a knot in my stomach—the same feeling I remembered from childhood when I'd hurt someone's feelings or done something wrong. Why was I voluntarily subjecting myself to this daily dose of negativity? I decided to experiment with a news diet. Day after day, I found something more productive to do during news time. I missed the adrenaline hit at first—that was the addiction talking—but I didn't miss that gut-punch feeling.

As days passed, my thinking became clearer. I realized how much of my thought patterns had been shaped by external agendas rather than my own values and goals. I was free from that toxic input.

Around the same time, I had a jarring experience at my church. The traditional Christmas program I'd always found beautiful and uplifting was replaced with what they called "A Christmas Holiday Revival." Gone were the poinsettias and ceremonial elements, replaced with stark decorations and performers dressed in black. The guest speaker made jokes about the Three Wise Men being gay because of how they dressed, asking what herders would "dress like that and hang out with two other dudes following a star." Many people walked out. I stayed, but something inside me shifted.

When I emailed the pastor with my concerns, his dismissive response made it clear: this environment no longer aligned with my spiritual needs. That was my last day in organized religion. I discovered that my faith was deeply personal—not dependent on institutions that seemed more interested in judgment than love.

The hardest part of my audit came when I looked at my relationships. Some people in my life were constant sources of negativity. They'd answer, "How's your day?" with a litany of complaints and problems. That familiar knot would form in my stomach. I realized I didn't have to subject myself to relationships that drained rather than nourished me. I could love these people from a distance.

This audit wasn't about avoiding reality—it was about acknowledging the weeds in my garden so I could intentionally cultivate something better. I had to name what wasn't working before I could change it. The odds had been stacked against me in the form of negative media, unsupportive spiritual environments, and toxic relationships. But once I acknowledged these obstacles, I could make different choices.

Life is what you make it. Life is what you seek. When you seek peace, love, and joy, that's what you'll find. Not that everything will be roses—but you'll have the clarity to see opportunities that might otherwise be obscured by the weeds.

So if you're looking at your own life right now—at the grief, the rejection, the stories you've been told about what's NOT possible—know this:

You're not here to prove the odds wrong. You're here to rise despite the odds.

Naming the Odds

This isn't about ignoring reality or pretending challenges don't exist. It's about seeing them clearly, naming them honestly, and then making the conscious choice to believe in your capacity to navigate them. True belief isn't built on denial—it's built on acknowledgment followed by determination.

- What odds are stacked against you right now? Name them. Write them down.
- Look them in the eye. How do they make you feel?
- Then ask yourself: "What's one step I can take today, despite these odds?"
- Revisit this list regularly. Cross off odds you've overcome and celebrate those victories.

That step, however small, is where belief begins to take root. It's not about proving the odds wrong—it's about proving to yourself that odds don't get the final say in your story.

If you're comfortable sharing your journey of facing your odds, I'd love to hear about it. Connect with me on social media and let me know what step you took.

Don't Believe Yourself Fully, Believe in Yourself Fully

How often do you one hundred percent believe the words that come out of your mouth—with no exaggeration, no BS?

What about your thoughts? Do you believe the things you say to yourself?

How often do you *truly* believe in yourself?

These are questions that usually stop people in their tracks. In conversation, they might try to clarify or double down, fumbling around for evidence, factual or not. I've learned from experience that this reaction often comes from a place of fear, pride, or pain. They are trying to convince themselves as much as they are trying to convince others because deep down, they know what they're saying isn't the full truth.

Remember my Life Audit? If I had fully believed the narratives I was telling myself—that I needed the news to stay informed, that my church was the only path to spiritual fulfillment, that I had to maintain relationships with people who drained me—I was stuck in thought patterns that weren't serving me. The breakthrough came when I stopped believing those stories but continued believing in my ability to create something better for myself.

I ask myself these questions too. It helps me to reevaluate my perspective when I want to believe the worst—or inflate my significance to protect a bruised ego—I stop and ask: *IS THIS REAL? OR IS THIS JUST THE LOUDEST VOICE IN MY HEAD RIGHT NOW?*

That check-in has saved me so many times. It brings me back to reality, where things are calmer, clearer, and a whole lot more productive. When I question my own narratives, I'm not silencing myself. I'm making space for *TRUTH* to speak. The truth about who I am. What I actually want. What's really happening.

It is human nature to brag, gossip, and talk with bravado, but that kind of talk does nothing to serve you in the long run.

You can't receive what you're asking for if you don't believe in it. And you can't believe in it if your inner world is built on shaky ground.

When we exaggerate, posture, or try to look more put together than we feel, we dilute our power. We become untrustworthy—even to ourselves. It's the "boy who cried wolf" effect, and once people stop believing you, it's hard to get that trust back. Worse yet, you may stop believing yourself, too.

So instead of believing yourself fully, start by believing IN yourself fully.

Believe in the part of you that tells the truth, even when it's uncomfortable. Believe in the version of you that owns mistakes, cuts the bullshit, and steps forward with integrity. Let that be the voice that shapes your story.

When you speak from THAT place, everything changes. Your confidence grows—not because you're puffing yourself up, but because you're grounded in something honest. Your decisions become clearer. Your relationships deepen. People begin to trust you. And most importantly—you trust you.

That's the magic that brings blessings to the life you're trying to manifest. That's what puts the *RECEIVE* in CONCEIVE, BELIEVE, RECEIVE.

Fail Up

On the road to success, failure isn't just a detour—it's part of the path. It teaches what success can't. Yet so many of us spend our lives trying to avoid it, terrified of what it says about us. But the truth is, failure—real, gut-wrenching, embarrassing failure—is one of life's most generous teachers.

I call this "failing up"–when a misstep becomes momentum. Stepping-stones to push off of and leap toward success.

Remember when I shared how I grew up with the last name Fagg in a small Texas town? Each day felt like navigating a minefield of potential humiliation, rejection, and bullying. I could have let those experiences define me as a victim. I could have believed the narrative that I was destined to be an outsider, that success wasn't meant for someone like me. Or even that being gay was bad, a sin, and that I was "asking for it" when people hurt me for being myself.

Instead, I used those painful experiences to develop resilience, empathy, and determination. Each rejection became a reason to prove myself, not to others, but to me. Each failure to fit in became an opportunity to define my own style, my own goals, and success on my own terms. I didn't succeed despite those failures—I succeeded because they taught me how to stand tall even when everything around me suggested I should shrink.

That's the heart of failing up. Every loss is a lesson. It gives you insight. Grit. In a way that success can't. Through this process of trial, error, and reflection, we improve our skills, adjust strategies, and ultimately succeed.

Look at Michael Jordan, who was famously cut from his high school basketball team. Rather than accepting that rejection as a final verdict on his abilities, he used it as fuel. "I have failed over and over and over again in my life," Jordan once said. "And that is why I succeed." That failure didn't just motivate him—it shaped his work ethic and resilience, transforming him into one of the greatest athletes of all time.

Or consider Thomas Edison, who reportedly failed more than 1,000 times before successfully inventing the light bulb. When asked about his many unsuccessful attempts, Edison reframed them entirely: "I have not failed. I've just found 10,000 ways that won't work." This perspective transformed what others would call failure into valuable data that ultimately led to a massive scientific breakthrough that changed humanity.

Oprah Winfrey, one of the most powerful people in entertainment, was fired from her job as a television reporter because she was "unfit for TV." She was told she was too emotional and not able to separate herself from the stories. Instead of accepting this verdict, she leaned into her empathetic approach, eventually creating a media empire built on authentic connection. "Turn your wounds into wisdom," she advises. Her emotional investment—once deemed a liability—became the cornerstone of her unprecedented success.

Tim Cook faced significant challenges on his path to becoming Apple's CEO. When he publicly came out in 2014—the first openly gay CEO of a Fortune 500 company—he acknowledged the years of struggle that preceded that moment. "Being gay has given me a deeper understanding of what it means to be in the minority," he wrote. "It's been tough and uncomfortable at times, but it has given me the confidence to be myself." His journey reminds us that our perceived "differences" and struggles can become our greatest strengths when we refuse to let them define our limits.

Whether you're embarking on a new project, chasing a personal goal, or venturing into a career change, remember that no one finds success through perfection. They find it through trying and failing and trying again.

So the next time you fail, which you will (we all do)—own it, learn from it, and use it as fuel to propel you forward and up.

Everything Is a Y in the Road

Every choice we make creates a Y, or fork, in the road of life. It's the moment where we're meant to pause, consider, then choose. But oftentimes we rush through, deciding without delving into the impact or possibilities of the paths before us. That impulse, that hastiness, can end up causing more trouble for us than we realize.

There is power in that pause, where all options are still open. This is the time for reflection. Take time to map out your options: the costs, consequences, and opportunities of each path.

This is where intuition begins to speak. Not the loud voice of fear or ego, but the quieter nudge of what feels aligned. The more we practice this stillness, the better we get at recognizing it. I've found that some of the best decisions I've made didn't come from pure logic or external pressure. They came from presence. From taking a breath, asking deeper questions, and tuning into what the moment was REALLY asking of me.

Because remember—once you've made a choice, you can never truly go back. The routes you could have taken instead will change. Circumstances shift. Other people make their own choices which collide and reshape what could have been, the moment you walk away.

But what if there are more choices than the obvious?

Sometimes our options aren't so clear-cut. Maybe it's hidden behind the brush or disguised as something less promising. It might not look like a road at all. These paths are easy to miss but are rich with opportunity. Creativity grows wild there—in the less expected places.

Can you make your own path? Of course, you can! You are the cartographer of your own destiny. You hold the map. You draw the lines. Blend two paths or lay a new road right between the others. You might not have to choose between the ocean or the mountains. Maybe there's a more scenic route that gives you both.

I faced one of my most significant Ys in the road when deciding whether to stay in my hometown or venture into the bigger world beyond McGregor, Texas. On one path was safety and familiarity—I knew how to navigate the challenges there. On the other was opportunity and growth, but also uncertainty and risk. What made this decision particularly difficult was that neither option was clearly "right." Each had its own set of consequences, opportunities, and challenges. I couldn't see the full path ahead on either road.

This is where the power of pause became my greatest ally. Instead of making an impulsive choice based on fear or excitement, I took time to map out what each path might offer. I considered not just the immediate outcomes, but how each choice would shape who I was becoming.

Ultimately, I created my own path—commuting between my hometown and Houston, getting the best of both worlds while I prepared for my next chapter. It wasn't one of the obvious choices, but it was the right one for me at that time.

When you face your own Y in the road, try this simple practice: Draw an actual Y on paper. On each branch, write not just the potential outcomes, but how you might feel traveling that path. What values does each choice honor? What growth might each path invite? Sometimes the right choice isn't about the destination at all—it's about who you become on the journey.

New paths are forever unfolding before you. There will always be another Y in the road. So make your map! Be your own GPS! Write up your pros and cons and make your discoveries.

In time, these brief moments of pause will guide you to places you might never thought you'd see. Give yourself that chance, be brave, and find clarity.

The Mistake of Thinking We Know It All

Imagine expertise as a dense forest. It's familiar and well-traveled, and you know every inch of it. But that comfort, that familiarity, may also be preventing you from noticing new branching paths hidden just beyond the trees.

To create, to innovate, we have to challenge the belief that we have all the answers. Expertise can be a double-edged sword. While powerful, it can foster arrogance. You stop asking questions. You stop being curious. You stop seeing clearly. Growth stalls not because we aren't smart enough, but because we assume we're done learning. Becoming an expert doesn't mean you have reached the end, it means you've been gifted the experience to ask better questions.

But that can only happen when you ground yourself in humility.

A non-arrogant heart is what allows you to hold your strengths and your blind spots at the same time. It doesn't mean downplaying your talents. It means using them while staying open to being wrong, to being surprised, to seeing something new.

I once worked with a team member who hadn't yet learned the "right" way to do things at our company. Within a week, they asked why we did our tasks a certain way. My first instinct was to defend our method—after all, we had developed these processes over years of trial and error. I had the expertise. I knew why we did things this way.

But something made me pause. Instead of launching into an explanation of our time-tested methods, I asked them to share their thoughts. "What would you do differently?" I asked. "How would you approach this?"

What followed was eye-opening. Their fresh perspective, unburdened by our company's history and assumptions, allowed them to see inefficiencies that had become invisible to us. They proposed a simple change that would eliminate three unnecessary steps in our process.

As I listened, I realized we had been clinging to a system that had made sense years ago but had become outdated as our business evolved. We had stopped questioning it because "that's just how we do things here." Our expertise had become a blind spot.

We implemented their suggestion, and that simple change saved us hours of work each week and thousands of dollars over the following months. That moment wasn't just about improving a process—it reminded me that fresh perspectives are gold, and that sometimes the most valuable expertise is knowing when to set aside what you think you know. This experience taught me that true expertise isn't about having all the answers—it's about asking better questions. It's about holding what you know lightly enough that you can still be surprised, still be wrong, still be taught.

Try this: The next time you find yourself automatically dismissing an idea because "that's not how it's done" or "I already know about this," pause and ask yourself: "What if I'm wrong? What might I learn if I approach this with curiosity instead of certainty?" This simple practice has saved me from the arrogance of expertise more times than I can count.

That's the gift of humility. It's not passive. It's active work. You practice awareness. You stay honest with yourself and others. You hold back from posturing or pretending, even when insecurity creeps in.

In a world that often idolizes wealth, status, and being right, choosing to be humble is a radical act. It may seem counterintuitive, but it's the choice that makes the biggest difference

Compassion for others is active. It is work. Understanding the struggles of others, seeing their perspectives, successes, and failures—that is where respect grows. But it's the one that makes the biggest difference. In humility, you keep your heart aligned with your values. You keep your actions grounded in truth.

As you grow, learn, and gain experience, keep that beginner's mindset.

- **Stay Curious.** Don't just teach—keep learning. Read. Ask. Listen more than you speak.
- **Invite Outside Eyes.** Get feedback from people outside your usual bubble. They'll see what you've become blind to.
- **Celebrate the Questions.** Especially the ones that get you out of your comfort zone. They're pointing to something that matters.
- **Stay Humble.** Growth is a forever process. Let that be exciting, not exhausting.

Try this mantra: I let go of my ego and discovered new truths.

So whether you're just starting out or are years into your path, keep asking "Why?" Be brave enough to say, "I don't know"—and humble enough to learn.

Finding Hearts in Flowers

I heard the song "LEAVE BEAUTY WHERE YOU PASS" by Lyra & Roark Barron at a Renaissance Festival in 1989. The profound lyrics and haunting music of these performing artists affected me in a way I'll never forget. Two performers in an elaborate Romani wagon playing chimes, bells, and more, carried a message of love and leaving beauty behind wherever you go.

It confirmed what I had always suspected about myself: that I had a knack for finding blessings and meaning in everything I encountered. That day was no different. I looked around at the beautiful landscape of central Texas. I was with lovely, creative friends who were supportive and loving. There was warmth in the sunshine after the rain, and a breeze carrying bright spring scents.

While Lyra & Roark performed, people danced around them, relishing in their whimsical music. Lyra twirled in her fairy gown as incense drifted through the air. It was like stepping into a dream or a movie made real. Everything was peaceful, golden, and bright.

I realized in that moment that throughout my life, I'd always believed things would get better, and keep getting better, no matter how good or hard it was.

I thought, "*WHAT MADE ME THINK THIS WAY?*"

I knew I had struggled in my life, but I'd always done my best to listen, learn, and take each lesson to heart.

While on a creative break from writing, I decided to take some time to paint with watercolors. With soft smears of color, a Texas bluebonnet began to form. When the paint had dried, I went back to the canvas, a fine black marker in hand, intending to add the outlines. But as close as I was, I discovered that one of the negative spaces between blooms was shaped like a heart.

Instead of tracing the bluebonnet's petals, I traced the lines between them, highlighting the little white heart. I sat back, inspecting the broader picture, and noticed other places with similar heart-shaped spaces. I traced one after another, finding more and more hearts between the blooms. I started to see other subtle areas where the colors shifted and revealed even more. By the time I was done, my canvas was filled with dozens of hearts, and the perspective of the painting forever changed.

It had been an assignment from my writing coach, Lauren Marie Fleming, to take a step back and "do something creative" to reset and seek out new inspiration. In that choice, I found exactly what I needed. Something clicked within me. I saw the bigger picture, but my perspective had changed. I saw the hearts between the petals, just waiting to be featured.

I have worked hard to build a life centered around what I want to be. Years have passed where I had to make choices, both simple and hard, to surround myself with people who inspire me to be greater while loving me for who I am. I have learned how music and movies affect the way I see the world and see myself. I've discovered how I can control how I am affected by all these things by deciding who and what I allow into my space.

These experiences taught me fundamental truths about perception and reality:

- You become what you seek, what you think, and what you wish for.
- Your perspective is shaped by how you listen, what you watch, and who you choose to surround yourself with.
- If you believe you are worthy, you will be.

This is the essence of true belief—not just thinking something is possible but training yourself to see evidence of it everywhere you look. We are connected to and affected by everything around us. It is how we choose to interact with it all that shapes our reality.

Living With Abundance

It doesn't happen all at once. Living with an abundance mindset is more of a remembering than a learning. It's a shift that begins subtly—maybe with a single choice. A moment when you trust something will come through without grasping for control. A moment when you give generously, without calculating the return. A moment when you catch yourself reaching for the old fears, then pause and let them go.

I remember the first time this shift happened for me. I was in the early days of building my business, constantly worried there weren't enough clients, enough money, enough time. I found myself viewing other entrepreneurs in my field as competition—people who might take "my" clients or "my" opportunities. This mindset was exhausting. It kept me in a constant state of anxiety and defensiveness.

Then my mentor, Tony Robbins, asked me a simple question: "What if there's more than enough for everyone, including you?"

At first, I resisted. After all, resources are finite, right? But as I sat with this question, something began to shift. I started noticing opportunities I'd been blind to before. I began collaborating with those same "competitors," and together we created more value than we ever could have alone. Clients seemed to appear from unexpected places. The more I operated from abundance, the more abundance showed up.

Now, I'm not suggesting that material resources are literally infinite. But I am saying that when you shift from scarcity to abundance thinking, you expand what's possible within the resources available. You see solutions instead of limitations. You create value where others see only what exists.

The first time I did that—really let go—I didn't even realize it. I was standing at a crossroads in my life, unsure of whether to play it safe or bet on myself. I chose the risk. And what followed wasn't immediate success, but a different kind of wealth: clarity, creativity, and community. That was the first ripple.

This is what abundance gives you. A ripple effect that starts from within and changes everything around you. It's not about the size of your bank account or the number of followers on your page. It's about the frequency you live on. The energy you put out. The trust you place in the unseen, and the willingness to move even before the path is lit.

Abundance is saying yes to opportunity even when it scares you. It's letting go of the story that there's not enough to go around. It's choosing connection over competition, celebration over jealousy, and expansion over control.

When you start living abundantly, people notice—even if they can't name it. They feel more relaxed around you. They stop bracing for judgment. They open up. That's the ripple. You shift your mindset, and the people in your orbit shift too. You walk into a room with nothing to prove, and suddenly, you have influence without effort.

You also start moving differently. Not with urgency, but with assurance. You no longer rush to the front of the line or panic when someone else gets the thing you want. You know there's more. More love, more success, more timing that hasn't yet arrived.

This doesn't mean you float through life with no action or ambition. Quite the opposite. You act boldly because you're not acting from fear. You take the leap because you trust the net will appear—or that you'll learn to fly on the way down.

And yes, sometimes that net looks different than you imagined. Maybe you wanted a yes and got a lesson instead. Maybe you wanted clarity and got waiting. But if you're living abundantly, you'll know to keep going. To trust that nothing is wasted and that every detour is a redirection toward something better.

Trusting the universe is a cornerstone of this mindset. It's the knowing that not everything is yours—but what IS yours can't miss you. It's about honoring divine timing even when your ego wants control. It's being okay with not having the full picture yet and still moving forward with faith.

I've lived both ways—out of scarcity and out of abundance—and I can tell you this: the world doesn't change when you shift mindsets. You do. And in doing so, the world reacts to you differently. Doors open that used to stay shut. People extend invitations you didn't see coming. You become a magnet for possibility.

But here's what people don't always say: abundance can be uncomfortable. It means receiving when you're used to scraping. It means resting when you've built your worth on hustle. It means saying no to breadcrumbs because you've finally realized you deserve the feast. And that kind of shift? It shakes things up.

Old patterns will tug at you. People who benefit from your scarcity will resist the change. You may even sabotage your own progress just to feel familiar. That's normal. But it's not a reason to stop. Keep choosing the mindset that affirms your worth. Keep acting as if what you want is already on its way.

Because it is.

You'll see the effects everywhere: in how you speak to yourself, how you hold boundaries, how you celebrate others without shrinking yourself.

You'll invest in things that matter. You'll forgive more freely. You'll let yourself be seen.

And perhaps most powerfully, you'll begin to trust that joy is not a fluke. That good things aren't just for other people. That life—your life—can be full of lightness, connection, and purpose.

That's the power of living with abundance. You don't just change your mindset. You change your entire experience.

You stop bracing. You start receiving. And the ripples never stop.

Make Your Own Luck: The Magic of Momentum

The question of whether luck can be created or if it's something we stumble into has been a debate for ages. I used to think lucky people just had something I didn't: better timing, better connections, better stars aligned in their favor. But the more I paid attention, the more I realized that luck isn't about waiting for the right moment. It's about creating the right moment. It's about motion.

Lucky folks—people who seem to be magnets for opportunity—are usually the ones who've practiced being able to recognize it, prepare for it, and act on it. They don't wait for things to be perfect. They move to meet the moment.

Look at Tyler Perry. Faced with rejection from traditional entertainment channels, Perry invested his life savings in staging his own plays. He built an audience directly, performing in small venues and churches before moving to larger theaters. When mainstream success finally came, many called it luck, but it wasn't—it was the result of years of creating his own opportunities and building a loyal audience that traditional gatekeepers couldn't ignore.

Or consider Sara Blakely, the founder of Spanx. While selling fax machines door-to-door, Blakely created her prototype using scissors and pantyhose. When she couldn't afford a patent attorney, she taught herself patent law at the library. She personally visited department stores to pitch her product. Her "lucky break" with Neiman Marcus came after months of preparation and persistence. What looked like fortunate timing to outsiders was actually the culmination of countless deliberate actions.

Lin-Manuel Miranda's journey with *Hamilton* tells the same story. Before it became a global phenomenon, Miranda spent years researching Alexander Hamilton's life, writing songs, and testing material at the White House Poetry Jam. What many saw as an overnight success was actually the result of years of preparation, research, and creative development. His "luck" was built on a foundation of consistent work and readiness for the moment when opportunity appeared.

Imagine you are standing on a tennis court, racket in hand, eagerly hoping you'll win the match. But when the ball flies over the net, you remain frozen, never stepping into position to hit the ball back.

Life works the same way. You have to move. Readjust. Even if you aren't sure you'll make it to the ball in time.

This is where the magic of momentum comes in. Once you're in motion, you create a forward energy that carries you toward opportunities you couldn't see from a standstill. One step turns into two. Conversations lead to more connections. New doors open that wouldn't have appeared if you'd stayed still.

This momentum works in every area of life. In business, a single cold call can lead to a meeting, which leads to a partnership, which creates a new venture. In creative pursuits, writing one page a day builds into a book over time. In relationships, one authentic conversation can deepen trust and open new levels of connection.

Even when you face obstacles—and you will—momentum helps you push through. Think of a flywheel that's difficult to start turning but, once in motion, continues with less effort. Your life works the same way. The hardest part is often just beginning, but once you're moving, each action becomes easier than the last.

The most magnetic people I've known are the ones who are the most present. They're curious, focused, and always following the thread of what excites them. They say yes before all the conditions are perfect. They take the class, find a mentor, and ask for help when they need it. And little by little, the rest falls into place.

This isn't magic, even if it feels like it sometimes. It's the result of steady progress, taken even in uncertainty. It's the result of knowing that you are allowed to want more and that wanting more is not selfish—it's deserved.

And yes, sometimes momentum looks like rest. It's about intention. It's about alignment and your overall well-being. Rest is an action. It keeps you moving forward toward your goal, keeps you balanced, and keeps you from burning out.

When you approach opportunities with agency, you create your own momentum. You stop waiting and start living. Be prepared, not because you've been promised a win, but because you believe that opportunity is coming.

Being in the right place at the right time might LOOK like luck, but in reality, that moment was preceded by countless decisions, efforts, actions, and alignment. That's the real magic of momentum—once it begins, you not only create your own luck, but you also begin to see what's worth holding on to and what should be released.

The Power of Love, Forgiveness, and Celebrating Yourself

There is a simple, beautiful Hawaiian practice called Ho'oponopono. At its core, it's about reconciliation and forgiveness that starts with yourself, using four key phrases: "I'm sorry," "Please forgive me," "Thank you," and "I love you."

I first encountered this practice at Tony Robbins' Date with Destiny event during the relationship day. As Tony guided us through various exercises to heal our connections with others, he introduced Ho'oponopono as a powerful tool for clearing emotional blockages. The room fell silent as hundreds of participants closed their eyes and repeated these four simple phrases.

What struck me was how something so simple could feel so profound. People around me were having breakthrough moments—some quietly wiping away tears, others with expressions of relief washing over their faces. I felt it too—a release of tension I hadn't even realized I was carrying. The practice wasn't about grand gestures or complex psychology; it was about returning to the most basic human needs: to be sorry, to be forgiven, to be grateful, and to be loved.

This practice teaches that healing doesn't start with anyone else—it begins when you acknowledge your wounds rather than avoiding them, and decide you are ready to mend them. Ho'oponopono encourages you to take responsibility for your experiences, not as blame but as strength. When you recognize that you have the power to heal your own heart, you reclaim control over your emotional well-being.

I began incorporating this practice into my daily routine, and it transformed how I approached difficult relationships and situations. It taught me something profound about love without judgment. The next time you find yourself in a conversation where your instinct is to react defensively, pause for just a moment and say, "I love you" to them instead. Even taking a breath and saying the words silently in your mind, letting yourself feel them deeply and genuinely before finally giving a response, can change the course of the encounter.

I put this into practice on October 11, 2014, in New York City. My partner and I had traveled there with two of our best friends to get married, since gay marriage wasn't yet legal in Texas. We arrived early at the courthouse to get our marriage license, standing in line behind two straight couples.

The man directly in front of us turned and asked, "Hey, are you guys gay?" As a shutter went down my spine, he smiled warmly and said, "Would you mind if these two gentlemen step to the front of the line? You see, they're gay and making a statement of love. We've had the luxury to get married forever. These guys have a new opportunity."

The couple at the very front agreed immediately, and we became the first gay couple to receive a marriage license that day. We still have the ticket framed in my office. This moment showed me what happens when people choose love without judgment—not just for others, but for themselves too.

When you radiate this kind of love, it affects everyone around you. People soften around those who don't expect perfection. They feel safe enough to be real. Healthy relationships are built on reciprocity, giving and receiving in equal measure, and mutual respect.

But finding that balance requires an element of caution. If someone is not able to meet us with the same level of love, or if they respond with harm or exploitation, it's time to step away. Boundaries don't mean that love is gone, they are simply a container for it.

This is where self-love becomes a superpower. I used to believe that if I wasn't constantly producing, constantly proving, then I wasn't enough.

That I had to earn every bit of rest, love, or approval. My uncle Bill taught me otherwise when I was young.

"Here are the keys to the Porsche 911 in the garage," he told me. "You have 45 minutes until that car has to be back. Your parents will never know you just drove a dream car. Enjoy!"

He taught me that it was not only okay to enjoy nice things and experiences, but that I deserved them.

"I am worthy, bitch!" became my private mantra in moments of self-doubt. Not disrespectful, but empowering—a reminder that I don't have to earn my place in the world through constant performance.

You can't give what you don't have. If you can't give yourself the same grace you'd give a friend, then that grace will always be shallow. Self-love isn't about inflating your ego or self-indulgence. It's about choosing to listen to a kinder voice when your inner critic starts tearing you down. It's forgiving yourself for not knowing better and learning from those mistakes. It's understanding that you deserve rest without needing to have earned it.

When you truly love yourself—all your mess, your pain, your growth— your standards for living shift. You stop chasing scraps of attention or tolerating harm because "at least it's something." You start asking for what you deserve, and believing you're worthy enough to receive it.

Try practicing Ho'oponopono daily. Find a quiet place where you can focus and center yourself. Gently close your eyes and repeat the four phrases:

I'm sorry.

I love you.

Please forgive me.

Thank you.

Say them out loud. Listen to how they sound, how they feel. Notice what thoughts or experiences come to the surface. Recognize that the energy tied to those thoughts is contributing to your struggle

Self-love teaches others how you want to be loved. How you treat yourself sets the tone for how others will treat you. It says, "I know what love feels like, and I won't accept anything less than the real thing."

You don't have to stay small. You don't have to shrink yourself to make others comfortable. There is nothing to prove. You just are. And that confidence, that compassion, shines.

Conceive, Believe, Receive Action Items:

As we've explored throughout Part Two, **belief isn't just a mental exercise—it's a practice that requires consistent action.** The journey from conceiving possibilities to receiving them flows through this crucial middle step: believing deeply enough to act accordingly. The following action items aren't just suggestions—they're invitations to embody the principles we've discussed and transform them from concepts into lived experience.

Choose one or two that resonate most strongly with you right now. Don't overwhelm yourself by trying to implement everything at once. Remember that small, consistent actions create the momentum that leads to meaningful change. As you practice these exercises, notice how your relationship with belief begins to shift from something you think about to something you live.

- **Practice Generosity.** Each week, identify one way you can share your time, energy, or resources. Whether as a mentor, a friend, or an activist, generosity invites abundance and creates the momentum needed to reach new opportunities. Remember: what you freely give often returns multiplied.

- **Take Care of Yourself by Setting Boundaries.** Reflect on relationships where you feel judged, disrespected, taken advantage of, or unloved. Say no when needed. Step away from what drains you. Create space for healthy relationships built on trust, support, and kind communication. Your self-worth is not negotiable.

- **Trust the Timing of the Universe.** When faced with a delay or setback, take a moment to breathe and remind yourself that what is meant for you is already in motion. Write down one lesson or positive outcome that might emerge from the situation. Let go of the need to rush. When the moment is right, you'll be ready to meet success head-on.

- **Create Your Own Momentum.** Identify one small action you can take today toward a goal that feels overwhelming. Remember that motion creates opportunity. Don't wait for perfect conditions—create forward movement, however small, and watch how paths begin to open.

- **Practice Ho'oponopono Daily.** Set aside five minutes each day to repeat the four phrases: "I'm sorry. Please forgive me. Thank you. I love you." Direct these words toward yourself, a challenging relationship, or a situation that needs healing. Notice how this practice shifts your energy and perspective over time.

- **Challenge Your Expertise.** Identify one area where you consider yourself knowledgeable. Deliberately seek out a perspective that challenges your assumptions. Ask someone with less experience but fresh eyes for their input. Notice what new possibilities emerge when you hold your knowledge lightly.

As you implement these practices, you're not just going through motions—you're rewiring how you relate to possibility. Each time you choose generosity over scarcity, boundaries over people-pleasing, or action over hesitation, you strengthen your belief muscles. You're teaching your subconscious that you're someone who lives in alignment with your desires.

In Part Three, we'll explore how this foundation of belief prepares you to receive what you've been working toward. You'll learn how to recognize opportunities when they arrive, how to stay open to receiving in unexpected ways, and how to integrate success without sabotaging yourself.

The bridge between conceiving and receiving is believing—not just in your mind, but in your daily choices. These action items are the building blocks of that bridge. Trust the process, celebrate your progress, and remember that each step forward, however small, is bringing you closer to the life you've conceived.

PART THREE

RECEIVE

Embody Affluence, Lead from Abundance

"Be a good affluence."

It started as a joke—a playful spin on the idea of being a "bad influence." Friends would tease me, and I'd smile and say, "No, I'm a good affluence." They'd laugh at first but then agree. They knew I was an optimist, bringing positivity into the lives of those around me. I lived in such a way that my connection to success and abundance was tangible. It brought opportunity to others. My mindset, spirit, and outlook affected the energy of every room I entered.

That's what it means to embody affluence.

To me, "affluence" doesn't just mean financial wealth and status. True affluence is a deep, unshakable abundance of spirit, intention, and presence. It's about cultivating positivity, love, and purpose—not just money. When we move through the world encouraging others to aim high and reach for their goals, the success that follows only builds, grows, and strengthens, as we lift one another up rather than knock each other down.

Living this way, people begin to see what's possible. You don't have to convince them. They just watch. They feel it. You become a mirror for their own potential.

For example, real affluence doesn't hoard knowledge—it shares it. One of the most powerful, tangible ways you can lead others toward abundance is by promoting financial literacy. This book is my way of sharing affluence with you.

For many people, financial systems feel like locked doors they were never given keys to. Talking about money, building wealth, or managing resources often feels out of reach, not because they lack intelligence or drive, but because no one ever showed them how. When you take the time to share what you've learned—whether that's budgeting basics or investment insights—you're not just giving advice. You're giving someone permission to take control of their future.

Affluence is a skill. And part of embodying it fully is helping others develop the confidence and knowledge to do the same.

Too often, people have been deeply ingrained with self-limiting beliefs about what they can and can't achieve. These beliefs act like invisible barriers, cutting off their potential. Their subconscious mind sabotages their success, pulling them back down into negative self-talk. It's a defense mechanism, born from trauma. Though it might have been necessary for survival in the past, it's served its purpose and now only holds them back.

That's why redefining affluence is crucial. Until you determine that affluence can be joyful, expansive, and full of purpose, you'll keep shrinking to fit into a box that you were never meant to stay in.

And when you do finally break free, past those invisible barriers holding you back, you become a radiant beacon for others to follow.

You become an affluence influencer.

In Part One of this book, you learned to conceive new possibilities for your life. In Part Two, you developed the belief necessary to take consistent action toward those possibilities. Now, in Part Three, you'll discover how to fully receive what you've been working toward—not just the external rewards, but the internal transformation that makes those rewards meaningful.

This final stage of the journey isn't about waiting passively for success to arrive. It's about becoming someone who naturally attracts and recognizes opportunity. It's about expanding your capacity to receive without sabotaging yourself. And perhaps most importantly, it's about using your success to create more abundance for others.

Are you ready to step fully into your power as a good affluence? Let's begin.

Gain Mentorship

Throughout my life, I've been fortunate enough to receive mentorship from some of the most remarkable people. It taught me early on that I don't know everything, and I never will. When someone shares their experience with you, you aren't just listening, you're receiving something sacred: wisdom that was earned the hard way, gifted so that you can learn without having to bleed for it yourself.

One of my most transformative mentorship experiences came when I was struggling to scale my business. I had hit a plateau and couldn't see a way forward. Rather than continuing to bang my head against the wall, I reached out to someone in my city whose business journey I admired. I didn't expect them to respond—they were far more successful and busier than I was—but I took the chance anyway.

To my surprise, they agreed to meet for coffee. That one-hour conversation changed the trajectory of my business. They pointed out blind spots I couldn't see and suggested a simple pivot that opened entirely new opportunities. What would have taken me years of painful trial and error to discover was handed to me in sixty minutes of honest conversation.

But here's what I've learned about receiving mentorship: it requires humility. To evolve, you have to acknowledge that there are aspects of yourself where you are lacking. Once I accepted this, I started asking better questions. Done sincerely, those questions allowed me to have deeper conversations with my mentors. I saw them for what they were, not just public figures, but as experts with truths that would transform the way I navigated through life.

The knowledge I've gained has been nothing short of jaw-dropping. It has gone far beyond what I could have found through public interviews and articles. There is an intimacy in a trusted exchange that allows for real pearls of wisdom. These can be a catalyst for the change you've been searching for.

Mentorship isn't about access or status. It's about your willingness to receive. You have to show up ready to be honest, build trust, and stay humble. Bring your strengths, but also your struggles. Your mentor is not there to sugarcoat things; they are there as a guide, to challenge you, and to help you grow. The more authentic you are in your questions, the more real their answers can be.

If you're wondering how to find mentors, start by identifying people whose path or wisdom you admire. They don't have to be famous or even in your field—sometimes the most valuable insights come from unexpected sources. Approach them with respect for their time and specific questions that show you've done your homework. Most successful people are willing to help those who demonstrate genuine commitment to growth.

Keep track of the insights you gain from these conversations. Write down the advice you receive in a journal that you can refer to in times of need. But more than that, take gifts of wisdom to heart. Let it be a guiding post for how to make decisions, lead others, or be a mentor yourself.

I, myself, keep a notebook like this. Over the years I have filled it with gems, gifted to me through meaningful conversation with mentors and experts alike. And to take my own advice, I want to share with you some of my favorite quotes:

- **Mary Kay Ash**, founder of Mary Kay Cosmetics: *"NO MATTER HOW BUSY YOU ARE, YOU MUST TAKE TIME TO LET EVERYONE AROUND YOU KNOW THAT THEY ARE IMPORTANT."*

- **Joe Vitali**, personal development expert and star of *THE SECRET*: *"YOU HAVE GONE COMPLETELY DOWN THE RABBIT HOLE OF MANIFESTATION."*

- **Arlo Guthrie**, musician and counterculture icon: *"EVERYONE IS A ROCK STAR WITH THEIR OWN TALENT AND ABILITIES. I AM JUST LUCKY ENOUGH TO SING WITH A GUITAR ON STAGE FOR OVER 40 YEARS. YOU'RE A ROCK STAR AT HELPING PEOPLE HEAL."*

- **Mary McDonough**, actress, director, and producer (Erin from *THE WALTONS*): *"THAT LITTLE VOICE INSIDE YOUR HEAD IS ONLY 10% RIGHT AND 90% DEAD WRONG."*

- **Tony Robbins**, #1 life and business strategist: *"I LOVE THAT YOU'RE CONSTANTLY FIGURING OUT HOW TO IMPROVE YOURSELF IN YOUR BUSINESS. I'M LOOK-ING FORWARD TO SEEING WHAT YOU CAN DO AT THE NEXT LEVEL."*

- **Joseph McLendon III**, renowned Neuropsychologist and peak per-formance expert: *"WE ARE NEURO-REPROGRAMMING*

OUR BRAINS AT EVERY MOMENT OF THE DAY. BE CAREFUL WHAT YOU LET IN."

- **Sean Callagy**, international lecturer and coach, founder of Callagy Law: *"SEE THINGS THAT YOU HAVEN'T SEEN BEFORE."*

- **Geri Jewell**, actress and motivational speaker *(FACTS OF LIFE, DEADWOOD):* *"I may stumble, I may fall, But I'm always getting up again, Whether it be Winter, spring, summer or fall."*

- **Norman Lear**, iconic producer *(ALL IN THE FAMILY, THE JEFFERSONS):* *"IT'S IMPORTANT TO BRING INTO PEOPLE'S AWARENESS THINGS THAT NEED TO BE DISCUSSED, EVEN IF IT'S CONTROVERSIAL."*

- **Flip Wilson**, legendary comedian: *"STAY EXACTLY WHO YOU ARE, YOUNG MAN."*

- **Debra Messing**, actress *(WILL & GRACE):* *"ALWAYS HAVE THE CAMERA HIGHER THAN EYE LEVEL. IT'LL MAKE YOU LOOK YOUNGER AND THINNER, TRUST ME, SWEETIE!"*

- **Bruce Lipton**, Quantum mysticism lecturer and author *(BIOLOGY OF BELIEF):* *"WHEN YOU BELIEVE YOUR 'I AM' STATEMENT 1001%, THEN AND ONLY THEN CAN YOU TRULY BE 'I AM.'"*

Mentorship doesn't end when the conversation does. That's only the beginning. By accepting help from those who have already walked their path, you can bravely and confidently take the next step on yours.

The best mentors don't just help you follow their path. They help you recognize when it's time to trust your own.

Pain Wasn't the Point—But It Had One

We've all heard the saying: "No pain, no gain." It's a phrase that's been diluted by repetition, thrown around in gyms and locker rooms like a mantra. But like most clichés, it exists for a reason. There's a deeper truth beneath its overuse. Pain—not just physical but emotional, mental, even spiritual—is often the architect behind the strongest, wisest parts of who we become.

This isn't about glorifying struggle. Life will deliver hardship whether we seek it or not. But when pain shows up, and it will, it's worth asking what it's trying to tell us.

I started working when I was sixteen years old at my dad's medical clinic. I wasn't just looking for a paycheck—I wanted to learn how a business operated from the inside out. I wanted to meet the adults who ran the clinic, the consultants, the vendors. I needed to see how they thought, how they acted, how they set goals and created outcomes.

What I discovered surprised me. At sixteen, I was still a kid, but suddenly I wasn't just observing, I was contributing. What had been theoretical became real. Each patient's eyesight, their care, their experience—it all depended partly on me doing my job well. This realization transformed what could have been just a job into something meaningful.

I decided to approach my work with a mindset I now call "In it to win it" or "Run it like you own it." I took pride in every task, treating each patient as if they were my personal responsibility. Their very eyesight and life depended on me. What I noticed was that every team member shared this same mission, in their own words. We all took it personally that each patient deserved the best possible care.

Yes, the work was hard. There were long days, difficult patients, and complex problems to solve. But I discovered something powerful: when you're "in it to win it," the hard work doesn't feel like punishment. It feels like purpose. The pain of pushing beyond your comfort zone becomes a pathway to growth.

Growth isn't the only outcome pain can bring. What might emerge instead is wisdom. Growth happens when we go beyond what we thought we could do. Wisdom happens when we learn why we were afraid to try in the first place.

In every journey, there's a moment, or several moments, where things fall apart. Where your capacity for hardship gets tested. You hit a wall. The plan doesn't pan out. The losses mount. You feel tired in a way that no amount of sleep fixes. And when you get to the point where you aren't sure you can go on, something greater starts to take shape.

You remember where you started.

You remember the early pain of seeing how far away your goal is—the sharp sting of discovery. You remember pushing through the grind, doing the hard work when no one was watching, and trusting the vision even when there were no results to prove it could come true. And then, in some strange way, you remember that it was those same moments that changed you the most.

Pain was not the point. But it had a point.

We often think success is the reward. But the true reward—the one that stays with you forever—is the person you became to get there. That's the part people miss. They'll look at your success and say you were lucky, disciplined, or blessed. They won't see the nights you doubted yourself, or the days you kept going anyway. They won't see the pain you carried, only the gifts you have now.

But you'll know. And that's the real payoff.

You don't need to suffer to deserve success. But you do need to show up when it's hard. Let pain shape you, rather than stop you. If you can do that, something beautiful happens: you stop fearing the lows, and start understanding their role. They become a teacher of purpose, not punishment.

Sometimes the lesson is patience. Sometimes it's humility. Sometimes it's resilience. But whatever the message, pain sharpens the signal. It cuts through the noise. And if you listen, it leaves behind something that no material success can replicate: the confidence that you are stronger and more capable than you thought.

There's pleasure there too. A deep breath of satisfaction. Of well-earned pride.

The realization of, "I did that."

You endured. You learned. You didn't give up. And now, you're not just standing at the finish line—you're someone new.

That kind of pride doesn't come from applause or a pat on the back. It comes from the grind, the ups and downs, the moments of clarity where you see just how far you've come.

The moment you realize you're not broken, you're building, you start to hold hardship in a different way. You see that every fracture was filled with something stronger than what was there before. Not tougher skin. Not just discipline. But trust. In yourself, in your strength, in your spirit.

You no longer measure success in what you've gained—but in how well you've come to know yourself.

So yes—pain has a point. But it's not to break you.

It's to build you.

To create space for the next version of yourself to emerge. To strip away what no longer serves, so wisdom can rise in its place.

You didn't suffer to grow. You grew in spite of the pain.

And you know what? You have the right to feel proud.

Embrace Your Inner Child

In the whirlwind of daily responsibilities and expectations, it's easy to forget the joy, curiosity, and wonder that once defined our childhood. As we grow older, the pressures of adulthood take over, and too often we become jaded, losing touch with that playful version of ourselves.

I've experienced this disconnect firsthand. For years, I was so focused on building my business identity that I neglected the creative, playful parts of myself. My house was filled with art—pieces my husband and I had bought together—yet I wasn't making time for my own creativity anymore. I'd worked so hard to establish myself as a businessman that I'd forgotten how much I loved to play, to create without purpose, to explore without agenda.

This realization led to a significant change in our home and lives. My husband and I decided to transform a room in our house into a dedicated art studio—a space solely for creativity and expression. We signed up for art classes together, reclaiming something we both loved as children but had set aside in the pursuit of "more important" adult endeavors. We made a conscious choice to not just be collectors of art, but creators of it. There was something profoundly healing about picking up a paintbrush again, feeling the texture of clay between my fingers, and creating without concern for the outcome. It reminded me of the pure joy I felt as a child when making art—before grades, before criticism, before the pressure to be "good enough."

It reminds me of a story about elephants I once heard. When elephants are young, trainers tie them to a stake in the ground with a chain. The baby elephant pulls and pulls, but can't break free. Eventually, it stops trying. By the time the elephant is fully grown and strong enough to easily break the chain or uproot the stake, it doesn't even attempt to escape. The physical limitation is gone, but the mental limitation remains.

Many of us are like those elephants. The constraints that once held us back—perhaps criticism when we were too loud, too sensitive, too weird, too much—are no longer there. But we still live as if they are. We've forgotten that we're now strong enough to break those chains.

The return to innocence isn't a regression, it's revitalization. It's the process of peeling back decades of conditioning to embrace what was never supposed to be forgotten.

Within your childhood self—before the trauma, before rejection, before you were told to tone it down or grow up—lives your most essential you. That version of yourself who felt deeply and dared to dream big. You, who knew how to play, create, trust, and express without apology.

So why do we ever let that part go?

Part of the answer lies in how we learn to speak to ourselves. Think about how adults often talk to children who are struggling or making mistakes. The compassionate ones kneel down, meet them at eye level, and speak with gentleness: "It's okay. You're learning. I believe in you." But somewhere along the way, we forget to speak to ourselves with that same kindness.

Instead, our inner dialogue becomes harsh, critical, impatient. We would never speak to a child the way we sometimes speak to ourselves:

"That was stupid."

"You'll never get this right."

"Why even try?"

Being kind to your mind means treating yourself with the compassion you would show a child. It means recognizing when your inner voice has become a bully and consciously shifting to the voice of a loving mentor instead. When you make a mistake, instead of berating yourself, try saying: "That didn't work out as planned, but you learned something valuable. Let's try a different approach."

This kindness isn't just about feeling better—though that's certainly a benefit. It's about creating the psychological safety your inner child needs to take risks, to play, to explore without fear of harsh judgment. Just as children thrive when they feel secure in their caregivers' love, your inner child flourishes when you provide that same unconditional acceptance.

Embracing your inner child isn't some soft, sentimental exercise. It's hard. It's complex. It demands courage. When you look back to your childhood, it isn't just joy and wonder—it's also grief. You'll likely meet pain you weren't old enough to name at the time. You'll remember the first time you felt too loud, too sensitive, too weird. But making that journey back, walking through those early rooms, and showing up for your younger self, uncovers something extraordinarily worth it: that pure and happy part of yourself isn't gone. You've only misplaced it.

Here's what reconnection looks like in practice:

It looks like *PERMISSION*—to move without purpose, to laugh loudly, to try something new and be terrible at it.

It looks like *CREATIVE EXPRESSION*—dancing like no one's watching, singing off-key, coloring outside the lines.

It looks like *STILLNESS AND WONDER*—watching ants build tunnels, cloud-watching, asking why without rushing to answer.

It looks like *TRUSTING YOUR INSTINCTS*—not for their perfection, but for their persistence.

And yes, it looks like *PLAY*—not as escapism, but as medicine. Play is how children process the world. It's how they build confidence, test limits, and explore ideas. The same holds true for adults who remember how.

Try this: Set aside the metrics for a moment. Stop asking what's productive, what makes money, what people will think. Ask instead: What made me feel the most joyful before the world told me to earn my worth?

Was it climbing trees? Building forts? Telling stories? Making up dances or silly songs? Find that thing again. Revisit it. Not to be immature, but to feel the freedom and joy of what your inner child still has to teach you.

To reach your full potential, you have to be whole. Leading others with wisdom, creating a meaningful life, and embodying a joy that radiates, requires you to be in conversation with the youngest version of yourself. Not just the wounded one, but the wild one. The honest one. The one who danced like no one was watching—because back then, no one was.

And when you finally embrace your whole self, down to the very first layer, that missing piece you've been looking for was there all along. In your laughter, your curiosity, your fearless self-expression, and in your innocence—not as naivety, but as truth, unedited.

You don't need permission to return. You only need courage. And a little kindness toward your own mind.

The Forever Agreement: Building Unshakeable relationships

When people ask my husband Keith and me what our secret is to a lasting marriage, they're often surprised by our answer. It's not about finding your "soulmate" or having perfect compatibility. It's not about never disagreeing or always seeing eye to eye. Our secret is simpler and more powerful than any of that: we decided to be together forever, and we built everything else around that unwavering commitment.

Keith and I have been a couple since 1994. Think about that for a moment—that's over three decades of life, growth, change, and everything the world could throw at us. We officially married on October 11, 2014, joining the ranks of married couples when marriage equality became possible for us. As I mentioned earlier in the book, we were the first gay couple to receive our marriage license that day—the ticket still hangs framed in my office. As a gay couple, reaching this milestone felt nothing short of miraculous, but our commitment to each other had been rock-solid for twenty years before we could make it legal.

In all these years together, we've had exactly five real fights. Not five per year, not five per decade—five total. And honestly, calling them "fights" is generous. They were more like brief spats that fizzled out almost as quickly as they began. Each time, we found ourselves looking at each other and thinking, "Is this really worth it? Is this really so important that we need to be upset with each other?"

The answer was always no.

Here's what we discovered early on: when you truly commit to being together forever—not just until things get difficult, not just until someone changes, not just until life gets complicated—everything else becomes negotiable. Every disagreement becomes an opportunity to strengthen your bond rather than a threat to it. Every challenge becomes something you face together rather than something that might tear you apart.

Our "Forever Agreement" isn't just romantic idealism. It's a practical framework that shapes every decision we make. When you know with absolute certainty that you're going to work through whatever comes up, you approach problems differently. Instead of asking "Should we stay together?" you ask "How do we solve this together?" Instead of keeping score or building resentment, you focus on finding solutions that work for both of you.

This agreement transforms the entire dynamic of a relationship. Arguments become conversations. Conflicts become collaborations. Problems become projects you tackle as a team.

The foundation of our Forever Agreement is our shared mission—a clear, mutual understanding of what we're building together and why we're building it. This isn't about losing your individual identity or agreeing on everything. It's about aligning on the big picture, the overarching purpose that guides your relationship.

For Keith and me, our mission evolved over time, but it always centered on creating a life together that honored both of our individual dreams while building something bigger than either of us could create alone. We wanted to support each other's growth, face life's adventures as partners, and create a home filled with love, laughter, and authenticity.

This shared mission is what led us to transform our attic into an art studio, as I mentioned earlier. We both loved creating art as children, and we realized we'd been collecting art but not making it ourselves. That decision to prioritize creativity together has brought us closer and added a dimension to our relationship that brings us both joy.

Your shared mission might look completely different, and that's exactly as it should be. The key is that it's genuinely shared—not one person's vision that the other goes along with, but a true collaboration that excites and motivates both of you.

One of the most transformative realizations we've had is that very few things are actually worth fighting over. This doesn't mean we don't have different opinions or preferences. Keith likes the house warmer than I do. He is more social than I am in most situations. I am more methodical in my decision-making; he is more spontaneous. We have plenty of differences.

But we've learned to ask ourselves a crucial question: "Will this matter in ten years?" Usually, the answer is no. Will it matter that we disagreed about which restaurant to go to? Will it matter that one of us forgot to do something the other asked? Will it matter that we had different ideas about how to handle a particular situation?

When you zoom out and look at the big picture of your life together, most disagreements shrink to their proper size. They become small bumps in the road rather than major obstacles. They become opportunities to practice patience, understanding, and compromise rather than battles to be won or lost.

Reading about our thirty-year relationship and thinking "That sounds nice, but it could never work for me" is exactly the kind of thinking this book is designed to challenge. Why not you? What makes you different from any other couple who has built a lasting, loving relationship?

The truth is, there's nothing special about Keith and me that made this possible. We're not more compatible than other couples. We're not better communicators by nature. We haven't had an easier path or faced fewer challenges. What we have is a decision—a commitment to make our relationship work no matter what—and the daily actions that support that decision.

You can make the same choice. You can create your own Forever Agreement. You can build a shared mission that excites and guides both of you. You can learn to put your relationship above your need to be right, to choose connection over conflict, to see challenges as opportunities to grow stronger together.

The question isn't whether it's possible. The question is whether you're willing to commit to making it happen.

Your forever relationship is waiting for you to choose it. Why not me? Why not you? Why not start today?

Building Your Forever Framework

Creating a relationship built on forever commitment requires intentional choices and consistent actions. Here are the key elements that have made our approach successful:

- **Start with commitment, not conditions.** Most relationships operate on conditional love: "I'll stay with you as long as you make me happy, as long as you don't change too much, as long as life doesn't get too complicated." Forever love operates differently. It says, "I choose you, and I choose to keep choosing you, regardless of what comes our way."

- **Develop a shared vision. Spend** time talking about what you want to build together. What kind of life do you envision? What values will guide your decisions? What do you want your relationship to contribute to the world? This vision becomes your North Star, helping you navigate decisions and challenges.

- **Practice radical acceptance.** Your partner is going to change over the years. You're going to change too. Instead of fighting these changes or trying to keep each other frozen in time, embrace growth as part of the journey. The person you commit to forever isn't just who they are today—it's who they're becoming.

- **Choose your battles wisely.** Before engaging in conflict, ask yourself: "Is this about our core values and shared mission, or is this about preferences and minor irritations?" Save your energy for the things that truly matter.

- **Assume positive intent.** When your partner does something that bothers you, start from the assumption that they weren't trying to hurt or upset you. Most relationship conflicts stem from misunderstandings, different communication styles, or simple human imperfection—not malicious intent.

- **Prioritize the relationship over being right.** Sometimes you'll disagree about facts, interpretations, or the best course of action. In these moments, ask yourself what's more important: being right or maintaining harmony in your relationship? Often, you can let go of the need to prove your point without compromising your integrity.

When Keith and I made our Forever Agreement, we had no idea how profoundly it would affect every aspect of our lives. Friends often comment on the stability and joy they see in our relationship, and we know it's because we're not constantly questioning the foundation we've built together.

This security has allowed us both to take risks in our careers, pursue individual interests, and grow as people, knowing we have unwavering support at home. It's allowed us to weather difficult times—job losses, family health crises, personal struggles—with our relationship intact and even stronger.

Our Forever Agreement has also deepened our individual relationships with ourselves. When you're not constantly evaluating whether your partner is "the one" or whether your relationship is "working," you have mental and emotional energy to focus on becoming the best version of yourself.

Become the Person You Were Meant to Be

There comes a moment in life when we realize we've spent too much time trying to be someone we're not—someone shaped by society, family, or our own fears and doubts. We hide parts of ourselves, conform to fit in, and stay silent to feel safe. But underneath that mask, there's always been a longing to be who we truly are.

This is the part where we pause, the journey is no longer about becoming (for now) but celebrating.

My own path to authenticity wasn't linear. Growing up with the last name Fagg in a small Texas town, I learned early to hide parts of myself. I carefully monitored how I walked, talked, and even where I looked. I became hyperaware of exits and potential threats. I shaped myself to survive in an environment that wasn't always kind to those who were different.

One day, a pink tie became my unexpected symbol of this journey. I was in my twenties, trying to fit in while simultaneously expressing something authentic about myself. When Mary Kay came in—yes that Mary Kay—she noticed me and called me "the guy with good fashion choice" because of the pink tie others might have warned me against wearing as a man in Texas. I felt both seen and terrified. She invited me to her seminar, saying "God is telling me you need to know what I know." She took me under her wing as an apprentice, to "learn everything she knew that she always wanted to pass along to someone." What she couldn't have known was that while I was wearing that tie, I was also hiding a fundamental truth about myself. I wouldn't come out as gay until I was 31, though I had known much earlier.

That pink tie represented both my desire to express my true self and my fear of doing so completely. It was a small act of courage in a world that often demanded conformity. Looking back, I see how even these small expressions of authenticity were steps toward becoming who I was meant to be.

My stepdad, Dr. Tennant, once told me something I'll never forget. After I shared my dreams of what I wanted to do with my life, he said," Yeah none of that's going to work. But here's the funny thing, intuitively I see, I don't know what it is, but for some reason I see you in front of a lot of people, on a stage and changing lives." Years later, Tony Robbins echoed this sentiment to me, reminding me I had an inspiring story to tell, and encouraging me to use my voice. Since then, I have stepped onto many stages—big and small—shared my stories and changed lives. I felt the power of living into the person I was truly meant to be.

But to get there, I had to reach a point of no return. Sometime in my mid-thirties, there came a point when I realized that this constant self-editing was exhausting. It was keeping me from the connections, opportunities, and joy that come with being fully yourself. I had to ask myself a difficult question: "Am I becoming the person I always should have been, or am I still playing a role to please others?"

The answer didn't come all at once. It came in moments of courage—when I chose to speak up instead of staying silent, when I pursued what called to me rather than what seemed safe, when I allowed myself to be seen fully instead of partially. Each of these moments was a step toward becoming who I was meant to be all along.

One of the most powerful practices that guided me was learning to hear myself—truly hear my own voice beneath the noise of expectations and opinions. We're often so busy listening to others that we forget to tune into our own wisdom. I began to set aside time to listen to what I really wanted, what brought me joy, what made me feel alive.

This wasn't about being selfish. It was about honoring the unique gifts and passions I was given. I discovered that when I followed what I genuinely loved—not what I thought I should love or what others valued—I found fulfillment and purpose. I stopped working just to work and started arranging my life around the things that lit me up inside. Art and beauty became central to my life—my home became what friends describe as "an art sanctuary," a physical manifestation of my inner values and passions.

When you learn from yourself and find what you truly love, you never really work a day in your life. Every task, even the challenging ones, becomes part of a larger purpose that resonates with your authentic self.

What I discovered is that normal is uniquely you—or as I like to say, "You-nique." There's no template you need to follow, no standard you need to meet beyond your own truth. Being yourself isn't just acceptable—it's essential. It's the only way to fulfill your purpose and live with the kind of deep satisfaction that comes from alignment.

You've committed to the work. You've made new discoveries. You've peeled back layer after layer of conditioning, fear, and self-doubt. You have reconnected with the essence of your purest self and become the person you were always meant to be. It's time now to embrace your uniqueness, express yourself fully, and step into the life you've always dreamed about.

It took courage and vulnerability to get to this point. Be proud of your willingness to let go when you needed to and push through when it was hardest.

Let yourself celebrate!

You were not made to conform to the expectations of others. You weren't meant to spend your life guarding your words, editing yourself, or suppressing your spirit. You stopped living for who you were taught to be and can now live as who you are meant to be. It's time to take off the mask you've worn for so long, and though it won't make life perfect or easy, you will feel the difference.

With your feet on the ground, you can confidently walk your path. You have brought home all your missing pieces—the ones you loved, the ones you rejected, and the ones you're only now beginning to understand. You hold them now in your heart and in your purpose, and you say, "This is me."

With your inner voice, outer choices, and daily rhythms all in alignment, you can finally, really, begin. When you stop asking permission. When you create instead of conforming. When you speak even when you're afraid to.

It takes courage to be yourself, especially when the world benefits from your self-doubt.

And yet, here you are—ready.

The Journey Continues

Staying true to yourself is not a straight path. It's full of twists, setbacks, and moments of doubt. But it's also full of joy, self-acceptance, and growth. It's important to remember that there isn't some final, perfect version of yourself, but that journey of becoming is ongoing.

Recently, I experienced one of those moments that reminded me how the journey never truly ends—it just evolves. Tony Robbins, Sage Robbins, Joseph McClendon III and I were in a private meeting. As we talked about the work we were doing, Sage said something that touched me deeply: "Don't we have a beautiful family." Tony added that we had a "front row seat on the healing and changing lives of humanity."

In that moment, I felt the power of what happens when you stay true to your path. It wasn't just about business success or personal achievement. It was about the mission—the real, tangible impact we were having on people's lives. It was a "wow" moment that reminded me that the journey continues to unfold in ways I couldn't have imagined when I first started.

That's the beauty of this process. When you commit to becoming who you were meant to be, the universe responds with opportunities, connections, and moments of clarity that confirm you're on the right path. But it doesn't mean you've "arrived" at some final destination. It means you're alive, evolving, and open to what comes next.

You should constantly be evolving, growing, and learning. Every experience, every challenge, and every victory refine you further. But to have gotten here was no easy feat. To refine yourself, you had to be whole again which takes time, patience, and effort. So rather than rushing, enjoy this journey. Celebrate small wins, new moments of self-discovery, and lessons learned along the way.

The wisdom you carry now, I encourage you to share it. Radiate it. Say yes to the things that excite you, even if they scare you. Say no to roles, rhythms, and relationships that ask you to shrink. Choose peace over performance.

As I look to my own future, I'm focusing less on exhaustion and more on smart work than hard work. I'm building community—creating sanctuary not just for myself but for others. I'm becoming more present in building my own brand and telling my story, not just supporting others behind the scenes. These aren't departures from my path—they're evolutions of it.

Your journey will continue to unfold in its own unique way too. The tools and insights you've gained through this book aren't meant to get you to some finish line. They're meant to equip you for the ongoing adventure of becoming more fully yourself with each passing day.

So, as we conclude our time together, remember this: The journey of Conceive, Believe, Receive isn't linear. It's cyclical. You'll conceive new dreams, develop deeper belief, and receive in ways you couldn't have imagined. Then you'll begin again, with greater wisdom and a stronger foundation.

Speak, create, love, and live like you matter—because you do.

Conceive, Believe, Receive Action Items:

Throughout Part Three, we've explored what it means to fully receive—not just the external rewards of your efforts, but the internal transformation that makes those rewards meaningful. These action items are designed to help you integrate the concepts we've discussed and embody them in your daily life. They represent the bridge between understanding and living, between knowing and becoming.

As you work through these exercises, remember that receiving is an active process. It requires openness, courage, and a willingness to recognize and accept the gifts that are already present in your life. Some of these practices may feel challenging at first—they're meant to stretch you beyond your comfort zone. But that's where true growth happens.

Choose the items that resonate most strongly with you right now. You don't need to implement everything at once. Small, consistent actions create lasting change more effectively than sporadic, overwhelming efforts. Trust your intuition about where to begin.

- **Peel Back the Layers.** Reflect on one part of yourself that you've hidden to fit in. Ask: "When did I first feel like this part of me wasn't welcome?" Choose one small way to reclaim it, whether through expression, acknowledgment, or action. Repeat as needed, until your whole self is brought back to the surface.

- **Celebrate the Pleasure of Growth.** The next time you reach a milestone, no matter how small, reflect not on the outcome, but on what you did to get there and what you learned along the way. Write it down and give yourself credit for how far you've come.

- **Practice Full Self-Expression.** Choose one area of your life where you've been holding back. At work, in relationships, or in personal life. Commit to making one bold change that is an expression of your authentic self. No apologies.

- **Create Your Sanctuary.** Designate a space in your home, even if it's just a corner, that's dedicated to what brings you joy. Fill it with things that inspire you—art, books, music, or tools for creativity. Make it a physical reminder of who you truly are.

- **Share Your Wisdom.** Identify one insight from your journey that might help someone else. Offer it generously, whether through conversation, social media, or creative expression. Remember that your experiences, even the painful ones, can be a light for others.

- **Plan Your Next Conceive-Believe-Receive Cycle.** The journey doesn't end here. What's your next dream? Write it down, identify the beliefs you'll need to cultivate, and imagine what receiving it will feel like. Then take the first small step toward it.

- **Practice Legal, Ethical, and Moral Decision-Making.** Before making any significant decision, ask yourself: "Is this legal? Is this ethical? Is this moral?" This simple framework, which I've used throughout my career, helps ensure your actions align with your highest values.

- **Be Rather Than Do.** Set aside time each week for simply being, not doing. This isn't about productivity or achievement—it's about reconnecting with your essential self. Notice how this state of being influences what you create and receive in your life.

As you implement these practices, you'll likely notice subtle shifts in how you experience yourself and the world around you. Pay attention to these changes. They are signs that you're integrating the principles of Conceive, Believe, Receive at a deeper level.

Remember that this work is not linear—it's cyclical and ongoing. There will be moments of profound clarity followed by periods of doubt. There will be victories and setbacks. This is all part of the journey. What matters is your commitment to continuing forward, to showing up authentically, and to receiving the full measure of what life has to offer.

The practices in this book are tools, not rules. Adapt them to fit your unique circumstances and needs. Create your own variations. The most powerful practices are the ones you actually use, so make them your own.

As you move forward from these pages, know that you carry within you everything you need to create the life you desire. You have the power to conceive new possibilities, the capacity to believe in your own potential, and the worthiness to receive all that you've worked for.

The journey continues. And I'm cheering you on every step of the way.

FINAL NOTE

The greatest love of all is the one we give ourselves.

That's the secret I've come to understand. When you believe in yourself fully and love yourself without condition, finally, you can be free.

For too long, we lived by a script we didn't write. We take care of others before ourselves. We dim our light so we don't outshine. We internalize voices that told us to stay small—don't be too much, don't get too big, don't stand out.

That kind of self-betrayal runs deep. It convinces us that survival means silence and that acceptance requires erasure. But once you see the pattern, you can stop playing the part.

Writing this book has been its own journey of self-discovery. There were moments when I questioned whether I had anything valuable to share, whether my voice deserved to be heard. The inner critic would whisper, "Who are you to write this? There are people with more credentials, more polish, more everything." But then I'd remember the core message that has guided my life: "Why not me!"

This isn't about ego or self-importance. It's about recognizing that each of us has a unique perspective, a unique journey, and unique gifts to offer. When I finally embraced that truth—when I stopped waiting for permission and started sharing what I've learned through both triumph and struggle—something shifted. Not just in how others received me, but in how I received myself.

You were created for more than conformity. You were made with purpose, intention, and power. Whether you believe that spark comes from

God, the Universe, or your own Higher Self, it's there—and it's waiting to be recognized. Not someday. Now.

Start with the one person who's been there since the beginning. You. From your first breath to your last, you're the only companion guaranteed.

Love yourself. Live for yourself. It's not selfish, it's sacred. It's the foundation for everything else. From there, you can see the building blocks available to you. You can start to build the life you want, from the ground up.

You get to decide who belongs in your life, and who doesn't. Who is truly family, who is truly your friend, and even whose soul aligns with yours. You may find that blood is not thicker than water. That your real family is not the one you were born to.

Your family should believe in you, love you, and support you. They are people who see your light and reflect it back. They don't ask you to shrink but encourage you to grow. They listen. They believe. They want all of this from you in return but don't demand it.

And you love them the same way.

Here in this place, this new alignment, the noise will fade. Doubt softens. You can start to rewrite the story you were given, this time with your own voice.

As our journey together comes to a close, I want to thank you for walking this path with me. For being open to these ideas, for considering a new way of being in the world. The fact that you've read these words means you're already asking the question that can change everything: "Why not me?"

Why not you, indeed. Why not step fully into your power, your purpose, your joy? Why not believe that you deserve every good thing you desire? Why not receive the abundance that's already flowing toward you?

You are whole. You are becoming. You are here.

I see you, I hear you, I love you. Because I love me.

With much love,

Scott

ACKNOWLEDGEMENTS

The first person who started me on this path is my mom, Marilyn Tennant. She was pure love, and she taught me to seek light in everything and everyone.

My birth father, Joe Don Fagg, taught me that today had to be the best day ever and that everything can be accomplished if you find a way. His limited time on earth showed me how to make each moment count.

I'm grateful to my whole family who mostly taught me good things but also showed me what not to do and who not to be—all lessons that shaped who I am today.

Very special acknowledgments to my Aunts and Uncles who are like parents, siblings, and friends all wrapped into one: Glenda & Bill Hart, Karen & Barry Houck. You've been there through it all, and I wouldn't be who I am without you.

Lauren Marie Fleming, my book writing coach, friend, and mentor—you helped me find all of me and direct it into powerful words. You pushed when I needed pushing and gave space when I needed to breathe. This book wouldn't exist without your guidance.

I've been blessed with incredible mentors throughout my journey, including Geri Jewell, Tony Robbins, Sean Callagy, Mary Kay Ash, Siri Lindley & Rebekah (Bek) Keat, and countless others who have given me wisdom on my path. Each of you saw something in me that I sometimes couldn't see in myself.

To my coaches who helped me level up in every area of life: Craig Baumohl, Charlie Mills, Otilla Kiss, Larry Mullne, Peter Hoffman, Mas

Mike Zeleznick & Maureen Miles "Vibravision." Your guidance has been invaluable.

I'm deeply grateful to the people who have trusted myself and Senergy Medical Group & Senergy Wellness. Every single one of you teaches me to be a better person, and I am grateful for your trust and care. You're why I do what I do.

To all of my friends I've met over the years who shared their inner thoughts, fears, dreams, and strengths—thank you for letting me into your lives and for being part of mine.

Marcella "Marci" Wallace Baldanza and Andre Baldanza (the Kids)— thank you for showing me how friends become family and change and enhance your life in ways you never expected.

To my incredible staff at Senergy Wellness: Jerry Gutierrez, Barbara Evans, Karla Bass, Tamara Bagwell, David Childers, Chris Gutierrez, Alex Zito, Deborah Lee Smith, and Linda Taylor. Your dedication and heart make our mission possible every day.

My Tony Robbins Platinum Partners family members—you have all taught me what true chosen family, accountability partners, and mentoring groups should be. The connections we've built continue to transform my life.

Unblinded—you all taught me to see what I couldn't see. I learned that your Ecosystem is key and finding others with thriving Ecosystems is essential to success.

Last but far from least, my husband, my lover, my friend, confidant, my soul mate, and partner in our forever agreement, Keith Yanick. You've seen me at my best and my worst, and you've loved me through it all. Everything in these pages is possible because of the foundation we've built together.

With each of these incredible souls in my life, I was able to find me, be me, love me, and reach for everything I wanted and be everything that I am. Why not me? Why not you? Why not us all?

www.ingramcontent.com/pod-product-compliance
Lightning Source LLC
Chambersburg PA
CBHW061430050726
47593CB00006B/2293